HOW DEV WON THE WAR

by
DEVIZES LOCAL HISTORY GROUP

Edited by Lorna Haycock
Photographs by Derek Parker

with contributions from
Olive Chivers, Arthur Cleverly, John Girvan, Lorna Haycock, Mollie Heath, Meriall Moore, Pauline Parker, Dora Seymour, Lorelei Williams, Margaret Worth

This book is dedicated to John Chandler,
who inspired us to begin.

Published by Devizes Local History Group
© Devizes Local History Group
No part of this book may be reproduced without prior
permission from the publishers
Produced by Create Publishing Services, Bath

ISBN 095 2548 704

CONTENTS

Part 1. DEVIZES GOES TO WAR   3
   Chapter 1. A Friendly Invasion   5
   Chapter 2. Devizes v. The Luftwaffe   12
   Chapter 3. Devizes Prepares for Invasion   25
   Chapter 4. 'Make Do and Mend'   33
   Chapter 5. The Community Spirit   40
   Chapter 6. Victory at Last   47

Part 2. ON THE HOME FRONT   50
   1. How the war effort was nearly sabotaged in Devizes   51
   2. Air raid precautions   53
   3. The role of Devizes telephone exchange   55
   4. The Mobile Medical Services   57
   5. The W.V.S.   63
   6. The Women's Land Army   65
   7. The Estcourt Street Post Office during the war   67
   8. War Weapons Week and other fund raising efforts   67

Part 3. REMINISCENCES OF THE WAR   69
   1. Devizes Grammar School at war   70
   2. 'Look, Duck and Vanish'   73
   3. With the A.T.S. in Devizes   74
   4. The butcher, the baker . . .   76
   5. Wartime childhood   82
   6. German prisoners of war and a baby   90
   7. Nearly shot in Devizes   90

ACKNOWLEDGEMENTS

This is the first publication of Devizes Local History Group, which was founded in 1992.

We should like to record our gratitude to the following bodies for their encouragement and financial assistance in publishing this book:

Gaiger Brothers
Kennet District Council
Lloyds Bank
Wiltshire Archaeological and Natural History Society
Wiltshire Local History Forum

We also thank the many people who have shared with us their memories of the Second World War, and particularly

P E Austridge
Marianne Baker
Heather and Mrs Benger
Olly Brown
D J Hair
Margaret Henley
Sidney Holley
Dick Hurn

Joyce Kemp
Pat Kennedy
Mrs A Nicholls
Janet Preen
Leonard Strong
Kathleen Wells
Jack Wishart

Thanks are due also to David Buxton, John Girvan, Bob Keepence, Wiltshire Archaeological and Natural History Society and Wiltshire Record Office for the loan of photographs and to Derek Parker for his patient and skilled photography. Devizes and Wiltshire Gazette kindly allowed us to reproduce photographs and advertisements from their archives.

HOW DEVIZES WON THE WAR

'If the Germans land, we can't, won't and shan't retreat. The battle will be fought out to a finish on the soil and in the skies and on the seas of Britain'.
   Ministry of Production leaflet 1942

Advertisement in the *Wiltshire Gazette and Herald* 25 May 1939

Part I
Devizes Goes to War

PUBLIC NOTICES.

GIVE THE WILTSHIRE T.A. A LEAD

MEN WANTED

4th & 5th Wiltshire Regiments,

In Trowbridge, Bradford, Westbury, Devizes, Corsham, Chippenham, Malmesbury, Wootton Bassett, Cricklade, Swindon, Shrewton, Amesbury, Salisbury, Downton, Tisbury, Warminster, Marlborough, Melksham, Calne, Bromham, Maiden Bradley and Mere (H.Q. Trowbridge).

217th Field Battery R.A.,

In Swindon, Cricklade, Wootton Bassett and Marlborough (H.Q. Swindon).

R.A. Ordnance Corps,

In Swindon as Blacksmiths, Coppersmiths, Electricians, Motor Vehicle Fitters, Instrument Mechanics, Welders, Turners and Lorry Drivers (H.Q. Swindon).

43rd (W) Divisional Signal Company,

In Salisbury and District (H.Q. Salisbury).

43rd (W) Divisional Provost Company,

In Salisbury and District (H.Q. Salisbury).

DOUBLE UP AND JOIN NOW!

Advertisement in the *Wiltshire Gazette and Herald* 25 May 1939

CHAPTER 1

A FRIENDLY INVASION

During the 1939-1945 war, the civilian population was much more directly affected than in the First World War. Air raids, evacuation, the threat of invasion and the shortage of supplies caused disruption and hardship. Whether they lived in town or country, whether they were in the front line or on the home front, no one could escape the effects of the war. In 1939 all able bodied men under 35 were conscripted. Women were not only conscripted from 1941 but also took over many men's jobs as well as looking after family and home, doing voluntary work and caring for evacuees from the large towns. Although not so directly affected as London, the industrial towns and the seaports, Devizes, which was the garrison town of the Wiltshire regiment and was situated near the Salisbury Plain military camps, became much involved in military preparations. Herbert Bolwell, who was in Germany at the end of the war, discovered a map of southern England on which Devizes was pinpointed. From the German point of view, therefore, Devizes was a legitimate target.

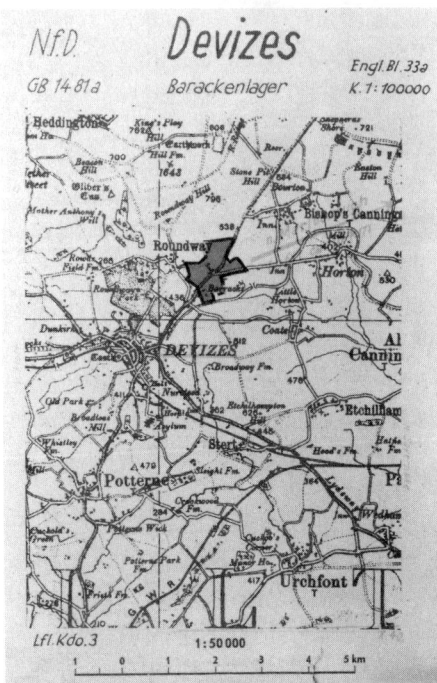

A German map of Devizes, highlighting the barracks

5

How Devizes Won The War

In January 1939, a National Service guide was delivered to each house, describing the various possibilities for national service – air raid precautions, regular and auxiliary police and fire brigades, first aid and Women's Land Army, as well as the fighting forces. Such was the enthusiasm in Devizes for participating in defence preparations that at a public meeting in February in the Corn Exchange to explain the civil defence system there was standing room only. During that year, the life of the town was to change drastically.

The first man to register at the Devizes Labour Exchange and the first to sign on at the Wiltshire Regimental Depot at Devizes.

In the spring of 1939, the Government ordered the construction of camps to accommodate the militia to be called up under the Conscription Act for six months training. Two camps with three parade grounds for 2,200 militiamen were constructed by Chivers on 90 acres of Roundway Farm. But first, because of the expected

A Friendly Invasion

military influx, a new sewer extension had to be laid from the camps to Southbroom, passing under the Kennet and Avon canal, with work going on all night. In July the first conscripts arrived at Devizes railway station in heavy rain, passing under a banner with the words 'Devizes welcomes you and will endeavour to make it a home from home for you'. Although some militiamen were housed at the barracks, most had to be temporarily accommodated in a canvas camp until the huts were ready in September, a wage dispute between Chivers and the camp labourers having delayed completion. Constant Autumn rain turned the site into such a sea of mud that straw and railway sleepers had to be laid to facilitate movement. On 10 August, the Chief of the Imperial General Staff, Viscount Gort V.C., visited the camps, describing the spirit of the young soldiers as 'amazingly good', though perhaps he had not been informed that 150 militiamen had protested at having tinned salmon for tea.

During the war years, British and later American and Canadian soldiers were to become integrated into the life of the town. The Borough Council had to consider how to cope with this military influx by encouraging the provision of leisure facilities. Due to the initiative of Toc H, the Corn Exchange was used on Saturdays and Sundays as a social centre where soldiers could buy stamps, cigarettes and cakes and post letters. The building was gradually equipped with dart and bagatelle boards, table tennis tables and

Militia camp under construction on the London Road, Devizes

Caption reads:
General Viscount Gort, V.C., Chief of the Imperial General Staff, with Visiting and Camp Officers, on a tour of inspection of the Militia Camps at Devizes on Friday.

Note the conditions underfoot

piano, and manned by male and female volunteers, who aimed to provide light refreshments and 'a homely atmosphere'. A soldier from Birmingham told one of the organisers, 'It is very kind of you ladies in this little village to help us like this'. The Y.M.C.A. also ran a canteen on the London Road and the W.V.S. set up a Services Social Centre on the corner of Sheep Street and Hare and Hounds Street. To keep the troops off the streets at night, the two cinemas gave showings for the first time on Sunday evenings, a move which caused some local disapproval. In November 1939, a milk bar opened in Sidmouth Street and 57, Northgate Street was converted into a servicemen's restaurant and club by the Salvation Army, serving egg and chips and sausage and mash and providing a room for writing letters and reading the paper. In addition, the

A Friendly Invasion

Wiltshire Gazette started an information bureau for miltary readers.

By 7 September 1939, there were 5,000 extra residents in the town, with the arrival of the troops and the evacuees from London. On 1 September, the first batch of evacuees, aged 3 to 14, arrived from Latimer Road School, Shepherd's Bush, and St Mary's School, Portobello Road, North Kensington. The evacuation arrangements had been made with military precision by the Town Clerk, Mr A. Hodge, assisted by the Borough Rating Officer, Mr J.E.Hopkins and Mr P.R. Trapp, the Clerk to the Rural District Council. Over the course of four days on two trains a day, 800 children arrived in groups of 50 with one teacher to a group. Every child carried a bag or cardboard box, a piece of luggage and a gas mask. They were taken to Southbroom School, the Grammar School or Southbroom Junior School, issued with rations for 24 hours and then assembled in the Corn Exchange to be allocated to their foster parents in the borough or the surrounding villages. A weekly allowance of 10*s*.6*d*. could be collected for each child under 14, 12*s*.6*d*. for 14 to 16 year olds and 15*s*. for over sixteens. Later groups of evacuees included a contingent from a London orphanage run by the Nazareth nuns.

The billeting process was not without complications. Some children had inadequate clothing for a winter in the country, especially the severe winter of 1939-1940, and the W.V.S. launched appeals for garments and shoes. A tribunal was set up in the town to deal with complaints about evacuees, for example that they were stealing from local shops, that they had lice or were badly behaved or were not house-trained. 178 evacuees had to be re-housed and 7 children were sent to the Children's Convalescent Home at Marlborough to be treated for 'scabies and bad habits'. 471 unaccompanied children were billeted in the borough along with 274 teachers and helpers. As a precaution, evacuated children were not allowed to go out after 7.30 p.m. Some mothers came with small children and rooms were taken for them at 36, New Park Street, Couch Lane and Verecroft in Long Street, for which the Town Council paid rent to the owners, with the W.V.S. collecting the necessary furniture, beds and blankets. Many wives joined their service husbands who were stationed in Devizes and soon

How Devizes Won The War

VILLAGE DESTINATIONS OF EVACUEES SEPTEMBER 1939

	Day 1	Day 2	Day 3	Day 4
All Cannings	50	15	30	30
Beechingstoke		15		20
Bishop's Cannings	50	35	46	40
Chirton		25		32
Easterton	50		30	30
Erlestoke		25		28
Etchilhampton		10		10
Great Cheverell	35		32	
Little Cheverell		35		10
Marden		25	6	
Market Lavington	100	75	96	94
Patney				10
Stanton St Bernard		15		14
Stert		20		4
Urchfont	50	50	46	50
West Lavington	100	80	70	70
Bromham	100	75	74	100
Marston		15		
Potterne	100	75	60	90
Poulshot		50		12
Rowde	50	75		46
Seend	75	50	70	70
Worton		35		40
Roundway	40		40	

there was not a single unoccupied room in the town. By October 1939 the population of Devizes had increased by 50% to 11,000 and consumption of water in the town had doubled to 100,000 gallons a day.

But during the 'phoney war' of the first winter, the evacuees began to trickle back; by 6 December, 435 had returned, leaving 309 in the town. In order to induce them not to return to London, the Mayor collected money to provide a Boxing Day treat, and parents who had come to visit their children were entertained to tea in the Town Hall by the W.V.S. on 17 December. Four days earlier an exhibition of evacuees' craft work had been held at Southbroom School. In subsequent years, New Year parties and film shows were staged. The continuing attempt to integrate the evacuees into the life of the town was demonstrated by the opening of St Mary's church fete in September 1943 by a seven year old London evacuee, Billy Jelly.

A Friendly Invasion

Until Easter 1943, the Ursuline High School, evacuated from Ilford in Essex, shared the Grammar School premises in Bath Road. They attended on Tuesdays, Thursdays and Saturdays, and Devizes first form pupils were allowed Tuesdays off while the second form were excused from school on Thursdays. Because women were taking over men's jobs, school dinners were provided for pupils and the Grammar School canteen served between 400 and 600 hot meals a week at 5*d.* a head. The first form at the Grammar School even picked nettles in the Braeside woods to be cooked for dinner. Playgroups were started to care for the children of working mothers and summer harvest camps usefully occupied older children.

When air raids on London and the seaports began in earnest in 1940, another wave of 500 evacuees arrived. By November that year there were 1,064 evacuees in the town, including 438 children, 21 teachers, 4 helpers and 426 mothers with small children, with a group of 162 from Hastings. Four empty houses in New Park Street and numbers 7 and 8 The Brittox were requisitioned to accommodate large families. 7 and 8 The Brittox housed an astounding 9 families, consisting of 13 adults and 27 children; seven families in number 7 had two gas stoves between them. Soon it was reported that the children had damaged nearby buildings and a bakehouse. When they finally returned to London in January 1942, one family owed rent and charges for light. The Billeting Officer tried to keep an eye on these difficult families from his office in the building and the W.V.S. started classes to teach the mothers to make and mend clothes.

As the air raids on London intensified in 1941, further evacuees arrived at the Grammar School in Bath Road which was being used as a dispersal centre. But again there was a slow drift back to the capital; by September the numbers were down from 839 to 527. The London County Council contributed £7 that year to the borough's Christmas treat to try to stem the flow, but the numbers declined throughout 1942 to around 200. Now there were new demands for accommodation for 500 war workers drafted into the area to do Government work. The pressure on the town's resources would not relax.

CHAPTER 2

DEVIZES v. THE LUFTWAFFE

Meanwhile, the town had been organised on a war footing. To cope with the expected dangers from bombing or invasion, Devizes acquired a system of civil defence. By the beginning of the war, a chain of command had been established, with a Control Centre in the Town Hall, manned by a rota of telephonists and messengers, equipped with a wireless and 6" maps, and under the direction of the military and the police. The Control Centre's function was to act as a co-ordinating body, collating reports from the air raid wardens and initiating the necessary action. The Borough Surveyor, Mr A.W. Jakeway, was the Co-ordinating Officer, and under him were 5 group controllers, 4 relief controllers, 14 female telephonists and 14 A.R.P. clerks and messengers. Should the Town Hall be hit by a bomb, the telephone at the Control Centre would be relocated at the police headquarters in Bath Road or the Estcourt Street Post Office.

At 10.50 a.m. each day, Devizes had to report to the County Control Centre on its state of preparedness and its progress in providing shelters, equipment and vehicles. On 2 September 1939, it was reported that the fire service, decontamination squad and the rescue, repair and demolition groups were in order and that a first aid post was being set up in the Bear Hotel yard in a lobby under the dance hall, though this was soon transferred to the Town Hall. Other posts, with a decontamination unit, were installed at the swimming pool in Colston Road and Lemon Grove in New Park Street. Equipment, such as stretchers and first aid haversacks, was stored for some strange reason in Short Street. Recollections of the First World War and the Abyssinian War were still vivid and much emphasis was placed on anti-gas training. Two years later, supplies of black cream were available free from the two chemists, Bawns and Boots, to be applied in the event of being splashed with blister gas. 25,000 gas masks, assembled by volunteers and older schoolchildren for use in the district, had been distributed by 3 September, though babies did not receive their 'gas tents' until March 1940. Two air raid shelters were set up and a complete blackout was established in the town by the time war broke out. Dr Waylen's appeal for the loan of private cars for transporting casualties met with a good response and the County Council allowed idle Local Authority vehicles to be requisitioned for civil defence purposes.

Leonard Trumper took over the organisation of the transport system, which was at first somewhat chaotic. Besides the Town and Rural District Council ambulances, emergency lorries and vans were loaned by local firms and coal merchants for civil defence use. Four could serve as ambulances and four could accommodate sitting cases. Of these, one had no petrol, one would only start on a hill and the ignition key could not be found for a third, though it was eventually discovered to be a switch on the steering pillar. During the day, when some of these vehicles might not be available, extra transport would be supplied by the police. Breakdown vehicles could be obtained from Nursteed Road Engineering Company and Chandler's garage on the Green. Under a scheme for emergency use of road transport by the War Office or local authorities, local firms were divided into groups, each with a manager who would ration work done by other members of the group.

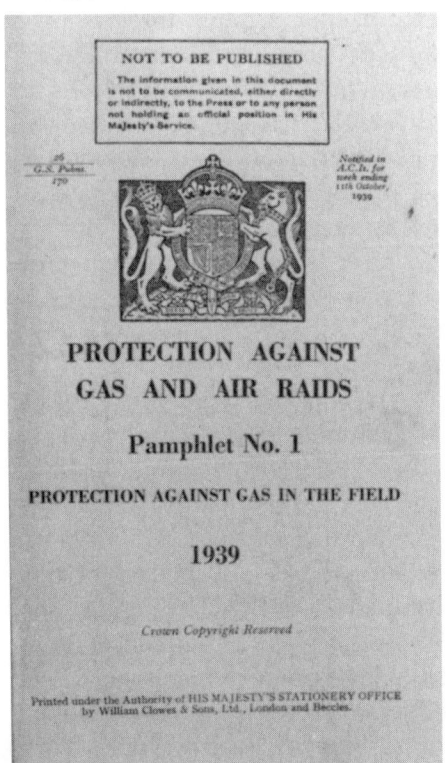

Although there was much enthusiasm to participate in civil defence and first aid work, there were many practical difficulties. Sometimes telephonists were not relieved at the end of their shifts and had to work extra hours. As most people were at work during the day, first aiders could only assemble *after* a raid had begun, when they would be collected by car.

There were three first aid parties, totalling twenty seven persons. At night one group, consisting of a leader and three assistants, was on duty from 8 p.m. to 6 a.m., initially sleeping in the Town Hall or in vehicles, using specially supplied blankets. The County Council, however, became concerned that civil defence personnel were not getting enough rest and that this was affecting their day time work. By the end of September 1939, therefore, it was decided that wardens and first aiders need no longer sleep at the Town Hall, but would be summoned by messenger in an emergency, though for a while in 1940, with increasing air raids, they reverted to sleeping overnight at the Corn Exchange, Another dilemma occurred on 11 September 1939. The first aid party could not find their kit. It was stored in a room at The Chequers, but no one knew who had the key. After some confusion it was decided to keep the key in the Control Room. A week later, the whole system of communication broke down because the telephone in the Borough Surveyor's office had not been switched through to the Control Centre at night. As the Assistant A.R.P. organiser, Mr T. Bullock remarked later, 'it was traditionally English for us to have stumbled through an initial stage of delay'.

Air raid wardens played a leading role in the civil defence effort. As the international situation deteriorated in 1937, an Air Raid Precautions Committee had been set up, later to become the Civil Defence Committee. The following year a qualified instructor was appointed to train air raid wardens and the rescue and demolition squads at twice weekly classes, including anti-gas training. In May 1939 the 89 wardens who had enrolled under the command of the Chief Constable of Wiltshire took part in a special exercise simulating an aerial attack on Devizes, with a practice blackout. R.A.F. planes flew overhead, with observers to report any visible lights. When war broke out the following September, the town was divid-

Devizes v. The Luftwaffe

A.R.P. map of Devizes showing the 13 sectors

ed into 13 sectors, with specified wardens' posts, marked by a plaque, for every 100 people. Wardens, who were attired in 'combination suits' with C.D. badges, received an allowance for the upkeep of their bicycles, 3s.6d. a month for whole-timers and 2s.6d. for part-timers. Sirens at the fire station in Estcourt Street and the police headquarters in Bath Road signalled an air raid, while hand rattles would announce a gas attack. The sirens were tested on the first Sunday of every month at 10 a.m. Air raid shelters were improvised at Bath Tramways depot, Offer's Corner and the Corn Exchange basement, as well as cellars at *The Elm Tree*, *The White Bear*, *The White Lion*, and Fortts and Parnella House in the Market Place. For all of these, steps were specially constructed. Although street lamps were painted blue to shield the lights, an S sign was left in plain glass to indicate the direction of the shelters. The notion of one Devizes resident that, in the event of an air raid, he would get in his car and drive up to the downs revealed the need for accurate public information.

DEVIZES PUBLIC AIR RAID SHELTERS

	In Charge	Accommodation
Bear Hotel	Mr G.W. Austin Mr J. Butler	74
Fortt Bros.	Mr W.E. Beedell Mr J.H.V. Lucas	66
Parnella House	Mr H. Norman Mr F.G.H. Armin	40
The Elm Tree	Mr G. Sheppard Mr R. Hassall	58
The White Bear	Mr S.H. Oliver Mr G. Young	55
Offer's Corner	Mr B.T.H. Skillman	70
The White Lion		62

Devizes v. The Luftwaffe

AIR RAID WARDENS' POSTS	HISTORIC BUILDINGS TO BE SAVED
44, Avon Road	St John's church
'Durleston', Bath Road	St Mary's church
1, Southview, St Joseph's Place	St James' church
1, Vine Terrace	Assize Courts
7, The Brittox	The Bear Hotel
31, St John's Street	Brownston House
15, Bridewell Street	Lansdowne House
'Spenwood', Pans Lane	17, Market Place
'Cleeve', The Breach	Old Town Hall
'Compton', London Road	Barford House
2, Bricksteed Avenue	25 & 26 The Brittox
6, York Terrace, Brickley Lane	14, High Street
Longcroft House	Parnella House
	The Castle Hotel
	8, New Park Street
	84 & 85, New Park Street (Gable Court)
	Northgate House
	Lansdowne House, Long Street
	The Rectory
	41, Long Street
	12, Long Street
	26-37, Long Street
	4, St John's Court
	28-30, 37-8, St John's Street
	St John's Alley

An Air Raid Precautions Book, price 3*d*, was therefore issued, listing all the available defence and transport services and the authorities to contact in different emergencies, such as damage to water mains, telephone lines or unexploded bombs. Bombs were to be carried to the Control Centre, (presumably with some trepidation!) and thence to Roundway Down for detonation by the military. During bombing raids, horses should be tied to the rear of their carts and not to lamp posts or railings. The handbook also contained the addresses of listed buildings in the town to be saved. There were hints on how to make a shelter and what to do in the event of air raids, incendiary bombs or gas attacks. If no shelter was available, it was best to lie down flat, as most injuries occurred above the waistline. Civilians were advised to remove combustible material from their attics and to keep vessels filled with water. A gas shelter could be improvised by sealing up windows and chimneys with wetted paper or sacking and covering windows with sandbags. Gas masks must be carried at all times – 'a man might become divorced from his wife or his job, but his wedding to his gas mask should not be broken'. Some people evidently found the carrying of gas masks irksome. On 19 October 1939, a Wiltshire resident wrote to the *Devizes Gazette*, 'An air raid won't descend on us like an April shower – I consider there is more fuss and signs of war in these country places than in London and other danger areas put together'. But the Control Centre was determined to keep people fully informed. A later Log Book gave further advice on what to do in case of blocked roads, the contamination of foodstuffs and the water supply. 'Don't panic' and 'Don't worry, it may never happen' were the general themes of these manuals and the public was reassured that the chances of being caught in an air raid were similar to those of winning the football pools, so 'Keep your chins up and keep smiling!'

'Put that light out' was a familiar cry during the war. To deprive German bombers of clues to population areas, a strict blackout was imposed. Shops had curtains at their doorways and all windows had to be covered with dark material, which was not rationed but on permit. Once when a window over the pie shop in the Market Place showed a light, a policeman shot at it and put it out at the second attempt. No cigarettes could be lit in the street and train drivers had to control the glare from their fire boxes. At the October fair, no roundabouts or sideshows were allowed because of the blackout. Problems arose when there was a full moon, which caused a glare of light to shine from the glass roof of the Corn Exchange and the roof of the gasometer. In 1939 it was found that the Control Centre at the Town Hall was showing more light than any other building because the blinds were not thick enough, so the lights had to be shaded. The offence of showing a

Devizes v. The Luftwaffe

Danger in the dark!

Lots of accidents happen in the black-out which don't get into newspapers. They may be trifling bumps and bruises — or something more serious. But all are a hindrance to the war-effort. So — look out in the black-out!

What do I do...?

I pause when I go out in the dark to let my eyes adjust themselves. I never cross roads until I know the way is clear.

I never flash my torch into the eyes of approaching drivers, and I remember I can see a vehicle approaching before the driver can see me.

If I drive, I take care my headlights are properly adjusted, and I drive at a speed appropriate to the limited range of vision.

Issued by the Ministry of Information

Space presented to the Nation by the Brewers' Society

Ministry of Information leaflet on the blackout

Devizes Fire Service 1941

light could carry a fine of £100 or three months' imprisonment.

Travel was difficult because railway station signs were painted over and signposts were removed to deprive the enemy of location clues. Moreover, there were no cats' eyes then on roads. Although car bumpers and running boards were painted white, car and bicycle lamps had to be shaded and torches covered with three layers of tissue paper; no bulb could exceed 7 watts and torches must always be pointed downwards. Not surprisingly, despite a speed limit of 20 m.p.h. in built up areas, the first road fatalities occurred in November 1939 because of the blackout. Dogs, trees, lamp posts and dustbins made even walking on pavements hazardous and in the country the situation was even worse. In November 1939 a Little Cheverell farmer was fined 5s. for driving a herd of cows 'on the highway in the hours of darkness without a white light being carried in front and at the rear of the animals'.

The hazard of fire from incendiary bombs, which had been much used in the war in China, also exercised the minds of the civil defence organisers. The regular fire brigade in Devizes consisted of 12 full time firemen and 4 firewomen, with 41 part time men and 8 part time women. They were equipped with 1 Dennis engine with a 500/700 gallons per minute pump and a Drysdale 350/500 g.p.m. trailer pump. In 1941 an emergency fire trailer pump was located in Rendell's yard in Long Street, with a 2,500 gallon steel water tank at Wick and a 500 gallon tank outside St John's parish room. There were 10 pumping stations throughout the town. The public was advised to use stirrup pumps rather than fire extinguishers; the possession of a pump should be advertised by a notice in the window to help neighbours in an emergency. Sand was distributed to various parts of the town for fire extinction and anyone could take a bucketful to use in their own home in case of incendiary bombs. Army petrol tins were released for civilians to fill with water and the Great Western Railway gave permission for water to be pumped from the canal into the Crammer. There were 16 pumping points on the canal and 25,000 gallons of water could also be obtained from Gallows Ditch pond in Hillworth Road. Arrangements were made for any furniture

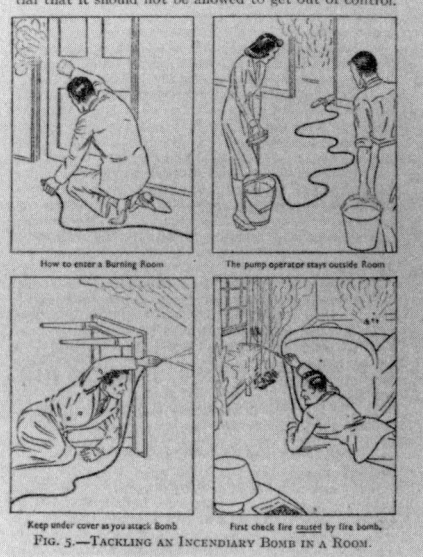

How to tackle an incendiary bomb in a room

Some A.R.P. equipment

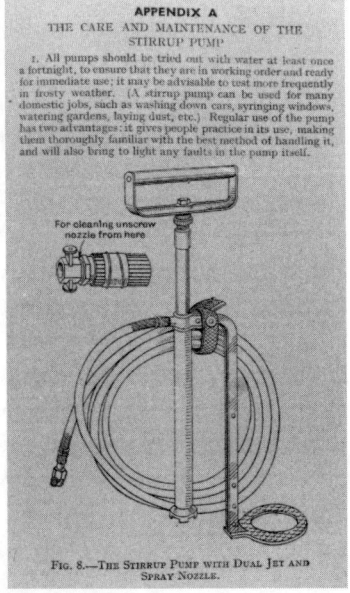

A.R.P. instructions on the care and maintenance of a stirrup pump

salvaged from fire to be stored in the front part of the Shambles, and bedding for emergency use was kept in the Town Hall kitchen, which was also to become a community kitchen if people were made homeless.

In July 1941 the town was divided into 3 zones, to be manned by teams of fire watchers. 85 volunteers quickly enrolled and even had a firewoman appointed to cook meals for them. A year later the centre of the town was split into 12 business sections, with 3 fire watchers to each group every night. Some 270 were regularly on duty in the town, being paid a subsistence allowance of 3s. a night. Shops had to display notice cards in their windows so that fire guards would be able to see where the necessary equipment was kept.

Devizes escaped lightly from war time bombing, despite being surrounded by military camps and airfields. After the fall of France in June 1940, bombs were dropped at West Lavington camp and in the Bromham, Tilshead, Melksham and Cheverell areas. Those that fell at Cannings, Rowde and Stanton St Bernard may have been targetted on the canal. Telephonists at the Control Centre had to deal with reports of suspected raids, which sometimes proved to be false. In September 1940, someone who rang in with information about 'explosions', which later were found to be caused by a car backfiring, was given short shrift by the telephonist – 'I told them politely but firmly not to trouble the Control with such trivialities and that I was busy with a *real* bomb.' In the same month a German plane crashed near Redhorn Hill and cattle injured in a raid on Seend had to be destroyed. Several German parachutes were discovered in the Patney and Erlestoke areas. A bomb near Baldham Mill in February 1941 left a large crater in the road, which a repair party quickly filled in to enable traffic to keep moving. One rescue party had a narrow escape while repairing a crater in the road at Coate; they later discovered that on the other side of the hedge there had been an unexploded bomb.

The only civilian death occurred on the first night of a series of raids on Bath in June 1942 when a council house was demolished in Silver Street, Potterne; an eighteen month old baby died and five people were trapped in the wreckage. The water main in Silver

Devizes v. The Luftwaffe

AIR RAID ALERTS IN DEVIZES

The first was on 15 June 1940 at 1.15 p.m.
The last on 13 June 1944 at 5.18 a.m.
Total number of alerts 164
Total number of hours 335 1/2
The longest was on 4 January 1941 6.25 p.m. to 7.10 a.m.
The shortest were on 5 April 1943 and 25 April 1943 – 8 minutes
61 alerts occurred in the morning
103 alerts occurred in the afternoon

Street had received a direct hit. It was feared that the heavy R.A.F. raid on Cologne in May 1942 would provoke German reprisals and everyone in the district was ordered to be alert, though the only unusual event was the machine gunning of a train between Lavington and Crookwood. It is to be hoped that passengers on the train had obeyed G.W.R. instructions to pull down the blinds and lie on the floor. During that Spring, first aid and rescue parties were sent to assist during the Bath raids, taking with them rations for 24 hours. The glare from the shells and fires in the city was visible from Potterne and Devizes. German planes could often be heard going to raid the midland towns and later in the war English bombers passed over to raid Germany and to take part in the D-day landings.

The coming of the 'flying bombs' in June 1944 brought a new hazard. Instructions were issued to help to identify these objects. They had a white 2' high six figure number on the right side of the fuselage and on the wings, tail plane and elevators. Any sightings had to be reported to the Control Centre. They also could be identified by the irregular engine noise, rather like a 2 stroke motor cycle, and exhibited a yellow or orange light before falling. When the Second Front started in 1944, it was feared that the enemy might try to impede the allied offensive by commando style raids on this country, so new instructions were given to cope with this eventuality. Code words would be issued by the military or by the Home Guard sector commander. 'Bounce' meant – Raid, Stand To, and 'Bugbear' – Raid, Action Stations.

How Devizes Won The War

For six years, Devizes volunteers played their part in the defence against airborne attack and a whole new organisation had come into being as part of a county and national defence system. Civilians were involved in their own defence for the first time since the Middle Ages.

Identification diagram of a flying bomb

Police secret letter about flying bombs 1944

CHAPTER 3

DEVIZES PREPARES FOR INVASION

The presence on the Green in the early summer of 1940 of hundreds of Dunkirk survivors, sitting still dazed after their terrible experiences, brought home to Devizes people the seriousness of the military situation. It was clearly now 'Backs to the Wall'. During the years 1942–3, the focus of local effort changed. As the threat of German invasion increased, an Invasion Sub-Committee of six was appointed to direct civil defence preparations and the Air Raid Precautions Committee became the Civil Defence Committee. At strategic points around the town, tank traps were constructed; these were holes with inset concrete and lids which could be lifted up for the insertion of heavy girders stacked by the side of the road. Signs to first aid posts were erected at Southgate, Estcourt Street, the hospital crossroads, New Street and Brewery Corner, and the Castle Hotel was designated an emergency hospital. The W.V.S. manned the Town Hall Information Bureau and a mobile canteen in *Black Swan* yard, and twenty women volunteered to act as ambulance and car drivers. All fit men between 18 and 51 not already serving in the forces were strongly encouraged to join the Home Guard, a body founded in 1940 and later described by Hitler as 'that band of murderers'.

The 4th battalion of the Wiltshire Home Guard, with a total strength of 366, was based at the Liberal Club in Devizes. As well as assisting the Civil Defence Committee in the event of invasion, three of the five platoons were responsible for guarding a particular area, with two platoons in reserve. The First Platoon, with its headquarters at Canal House, protected the Town Bridge and would man machine gun posts at Sussex House and Braeside. Platoon 2, based at *The New Inn* (later *The Southgate Inn*), guard-

A Home Guard platoon with dispatch riders

ed the Hillworth and Potterne Road railway bridges. The third, located at *The Rising Sun*, was responsible for the Sidmouth Street and Hare and Hounds Street road blocks, where they examined the identity cards of all comers. In an emergency Devizes Castle would be the responsibility of Platoon 4. Regular instruction classes were held at the Drill Hall, with firing practices at Semington and King's Play Hill and exercises in and around the town. At one such operation near Sussex House, a Home Guard fired a dummy round at a colleague and shouted, ' I got you. You're dead!' But all citizens were expected to play their part in combating an enemy invasion. The Government exhorted 'every stout-hearted citizen' to use all his powers to hinder and frustrate invading soldiers. Civilians could assist by filling in bomb craters, digging trenches, providing billets for troops or bombed out neighbours, helping with first aid or distributing food.

The official Government policy 'Stand Firm' would be carried out in two parts. Detailed instructions to this effect were issued in July 1942. When 'Stand To' was announced, the local Invasion Committee must prepare for the worst. All road journeys would be controlled so as not to impede the movement of British troops, and vehicles which might be seized and used by the enemy were to be immobilised. Although twelve notice boards were scattered round the town, notices must not be displayed which might help

Devizes Prepares for Invasion

One of the pill boxes built by Chivers along the Kennet and Avon canal as a line of defence against invasion. This pill box at Rotherstone was referred to by the locals as 'the block house'.

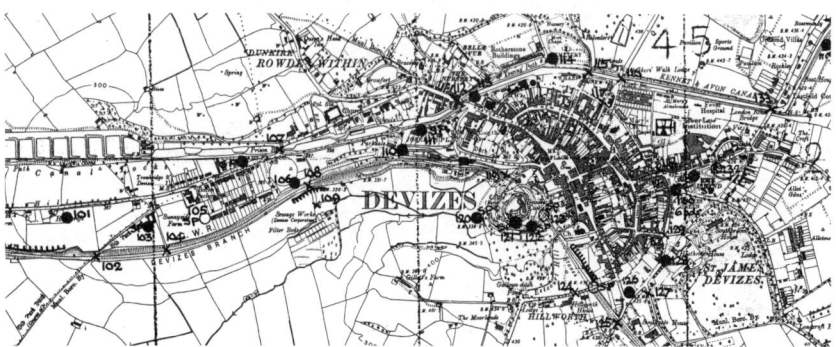

Pill box locations

the enemy. Instead, loudspeaker vans would tour the streets to keep the public informed. Once an invasion got under way and 'Action Stations' was proclaimed, suspects would be arrested and public entertainment banned. Roads would be closed to non-military traffic and emergency labels bearing a yellow triangle would be issued to be displayed on the windscreens of emergency vehicles belonging to the police, ambulance, rescue and fire services and the Petroleum Board. Police had the power to stop non-essential vehicles and immobilise them on the spot, including even pedal cycles. Post office personnel and barges coming along the canal might need to be decontaminated if they had been exposed to gas. Arrangements were made to stem the expected flood of refugees. They would be diverted off the roads into woods or on to the downs or at least kept to the perimeter of the town. Certain Devizes houses were earmarked to be evacuated if fighting took place in the streets.

AREAS TO BE EVACUATED IN THE EVENT OF STREET FIGHTING

Bath Road – Shanes Castle, Avalon, Hillsborough, Clifton Villas
　　　　　　Sussex House, Farleigh Place, Melbourne Place
　　　　　　12-15 & 22-36 The Nursery

Northgate Street – Canal House, Cyprus Terrace, *The Artichoke*

9 & 10, Southbroom Road
Pans Lane, Southgate, Wick Lane
Potterne Road – *The New Inn* to The Fairway
31, Long Street, Hillworth Road

Southbroom Cottage to Brickley Lane
Estcourt Street – the Fire Station to the London Road bridge
Sidmouth Street – Rose's to *The Rising Sun*

Devizes Prepares for Invasion

Detailed plans were drawn up for feeding and accommodating the homeless. The Devizes bakers were divided into three groups, each with a leader. If any baker in the group was unable to produce bread because of damage to his premises, the others would do it for him. If several bakeries were out of action, the Local Bread Officer would ask the Assistant Bread Officer at Swindon to import supplies which could be collected by bakers from the Co-op or the Mental Hospital. Each of the 14 grocers in the town would be responsible for distributing reserve rations for their particular area.

RESERVE RATION DISPERSAL POINTS

L. Sheppard } F.W.Eden }	Bath Road area
A.E.Cummins	The Nursery & Rotherstone
Co-op	New Park Street, Northgate Street, St Joseph's Place
Fortt Bros.	2 The Market Place, The Little Brittox, Station Road
Walkers Stores	Monday Market Street, Vales Lane, Park Road, Sheep Street Courts
T.C.Lewis	Commercial Road, Gains Lane, Sidmouth Street, Sheep Street, Maryport Street
Figgins Stores	Estcourt Street, Southbroom Place, London Road, The Island, Church Walk
W.C.Hand	Nursteed Road, Bricksteed Avenue, Brickley Lane, Meadow Drive
Alf's Stores	Brickley Lane, Kingsley Gardens, Roseland Avenue
R.Cave	Longcroft Road & Avenue
F.J.Barlow	Southbroom Road, Southend, Hare & Hounds Street, Bridewell Street
G.Sheppard	Morris Lane, Hillworth, Hartmoor, Old Park, Long Street
International Stores	Wine Street, St John's Street, High Street, The Brittox, Pans Lane, Wick, The Fairway, Potterne Road, The Breach

Lists were drawn up of 15 establishments which could provide facilities for feeding the population, ranging from *The Bear Hotel* with 49 places to *The Green Parrot* in High Street with 19.

CATERING ESTABLISHMENTS FOR EMERGENCY FEEDING

	Seating	Heating
Cross Keys, Monday Market St.	24	Coal
Hiscock's Cafe, 79, New Park St.	20	Coal
Robbins' Cafe, 50, New Park St.	20	Oil & Gas
Central Cafe, 5, Market Place	36	Steam & Gas
Bear Hotel	49	Coal
King & Trumper, Sidmouth St.	20	Gas
Cafe Rendez-Vous, 20, The Brittox	70	Gas & Electricity Bakery with oven
Castle Hotel	100	Steam & Gas
Strongs	66	Gas Bakery
The Green Parrot, High St.	19	Coal
Bancroft House, Monday Market St.	28	Gas & Electricity
Moonrakers Hotel	24	Steam
The Bell, Estcourt St.	16	Coal & Electricity
Chivers, Estcourt St.	70	Gas
Borough Restaurant, Market Place	90	Gas & Coal

If large areas of the town were destroyed, communal feeding might be necessary in the Corn Exchange and the Shambles. Eleven farms around Devizes could provide cattle for slaughter in the six slaughterhouses, and four farmers offered 22 cows for milking.

Emergency rest centres would be set up to sleep 300 at Southbroom Junior School on the Green, the Scout Hall in Southbroom Road and the Masonic Hall in Morris Lane, using equipment such as mattresses, towels and blankets stored in the Servicemen's Club and the Masonic Hall. Any salvaged furniture would be stored in May's warehouse in Northgate Street.

Devizes Prepares for Invasion

Temporary sanitation consisting of buckets and screens would be provided if many houses were destroyed. In the event of contamination of the water supply, water could be drawn from wells at Ansties, Wadworths, Chivers' works and sawmill and British Rola in Pans Lane. Chemicals would be available from the Gas Works for purifying water. Emergency fuel supplies could be obtained from various depots, coal at Devizes Wharf, wood from Chivers, candles from Stratton Sons and Mead and paraffin from the Petroleum Board in Station Yard.

If the first aid post was destroyed, an emergency dressing station would be set up at the Regal Cinema and the W.V.S. would organise a house to house collection of bedding and bandage material. Premises adjacent to Hillworth House would be requisitioned to accommodate infectious cases. Anyone splashed with liquid gas should go to one of the 29 houses displaying a 'gas cleansing' card. In the event of large civilian casualties, space was set aside at the cemetery for 200 bodies in 48 graves, and equipment such as shrouds and clothing bags were ordered for use at St James' Hospital mortuary, the Cottage Hospital and the garage behind Way's Motors in New Park Street. Police would exhibit a list of casualties and inform the relatives.

Various scenarios were envisaged, from the repulse of an enemy attack to occupation of the town by the Germans who subsequently advanced elsewhere. If Devizes residents captured an enemy soldier, they should disarm him, empty his pockets and take him to be guarded by the police in the basement of the Town Hall, handing over any maps and papers to the military. If the army advised that the town could not be held against the Germans, the population should collect food and disperse, hiding all papers and compasses and immobilising, though not destroying, machinery and spare parts which might be needed later. If a counter-attack was mounted, military reinforcements would rendez-vous at Braeside. Five cattle drovers would divert any livestock stampeding on the roads into the fields.

If the enemy moved on after occupying the town, people should be set to work in order to restore their morale, clearing the wounded, making bandages from sheets and burying the dead. Debris would be removed to Spitalcroft or the Nursteed Road tip, and parties would be organised by the military to begin the work of repair and reconstruction. Local volunteers would report to the Wharf where they would be issued with picks and shovels and organised in groups each under a charge hand to use building materials held by the Borough Council and local building firms. Devizes garages and coal merchants would provide the necessary vans and lorries through the Traffic Officer and nine farms offered carts and horses. Each building firm would provide an agreed number of skilled tradesmen. Chivers, for example, could supply 15 carpenters, 2 electricians, 2 bricklayers, 1 engineer and 6 fitters as well as 18 labourers. The whole exercise would be directed by the Chairman of the Civil Defence Committee.

Fortunately none of these possibilities materialised. For those lucky enough to escape the loss of a son, husband, fiancé or brother in the war, the main hardships stemmed, not from domination by an invader, but from social and material privations.

LOCAL RESOURCES FOR RECONSTRUCTION WORK

Employment Exchange	179 men & 110 women
Chivers	15 carpenters 2 electricians 2 bricklayers 1 engineer 6 fitters 18 labourers
Rendells	6 carpenters 4 bricklayers 3 fitters 17 labourers
Wadworths	20 labourers
English Flax Ltd	40 labourers
T H White Ltd	8 fitters
British Rola Ltd	6 engineers 2 electricians 10 fitters 12 labourers
Maslens	3 carpenters 4 bricklayers 2 fitters 3 labourers

CHAPTER 4

'MAKE DO AND MEND'

The years 1939-1945 were characterised by queues, shortages and improvisation on the home front. The submarine blockade and the concentration on the war effort resulted in rationing and inadequate supplies. The first commodities to be rationed were bacon, butter and sugar; cheese and meat soon followed. Everyone had to register with a particular butcher and grocer and was issued with a ration book containing coupons. Retailers' goods often ran out; news of the arrival of fresh supplies spread through the town like wildfire. There were long queues in the Little Brittox for fish and at the pork butchers' in Maryport Street for sausages. Fish, particularly sought after to supplement the meagre meat ration, was difficult to obtain because of the dangerous conditions at sea. Later, in 1943, salt fish from Canada and Newfoundland went on sale to make up for the shortage of fresh fish, which could only be sold near where it was landed instead of being sent on long journeys. Strange goods like dried eggs and snoek became staple items in the diet, and some even tried rook pie. The Ministry of Food regularly advertised nourishing recipes, using basic foodstuffs and instructions how for example to convert a dried egg into a fresh one by adding 2 tablespoons of water to 1 of powder. Many goods were 'zoned', so there was less choice in commodities like cereals. Occasionally goods were released by the Ministry of Food when they reached the end of their shelf life, such as sugar that had gone lumpy. Extra sugar was available for the winter feeding of bees and also for making marmalade, but only with proof that oranges had been bought. Under the National Milk Scheme, started in June 1940, expectant mothers and children up to 5 years were allowed a pint of free milk a day. An extra cheese ration was given to heavy workers such as the Land Army, tractor drivers and agricultural workers.

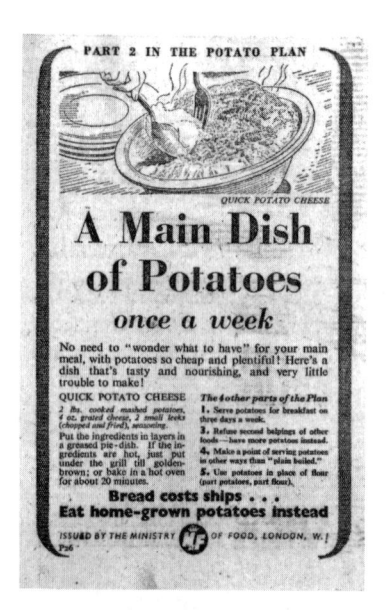

Ministry of Food advertisement in the *Wiltshire Gazette* 25 February 1943

Ministry of Food advertisement in the *Wiltshire Gazette* 4 February 1943

'Make Do and Mend'

Ministry of Fuel and Power advertisement in the *Wiltshire Gazette* 7 January 1943

Ministry of Fuel and Power advertisement in the *Wiltshire Gazette* 18 February 1943

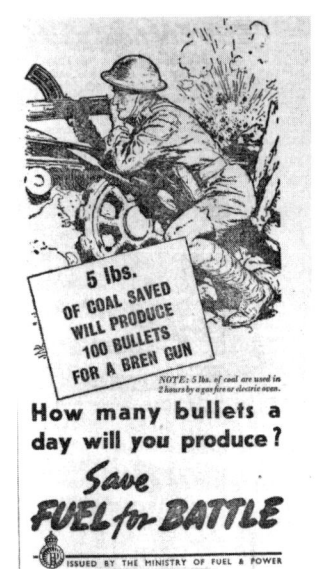

Clothing ration book

Ministry of Fuel and Power advertisement in the *Wiltshire Gazette* 16 December 1943

How Devizes Won The War

Bananas were unknown and oranges were like gold dust. Pat Kennedy recalls the plaintive question one Tuesday to the fruiterer on Gaigers' corner. 'Any oranges?' 'No, but we'll have some tomorrow afternoon', answered the shopkeeper. 'But you'll be closed then!' (Wednesday was early closing day). 'Yes, thank God!' came the reply. At one auction in the town in aid of the war effort, the Recorder of Devizes announced the sale of 'something oral and desirable'; it was a lemon and fetched 10s. (50p). Queues formed at Hams bakery in Sidmouth Street for cakes, though they tasted like sawdust because of the inadequate ingredients, and even bread was rationed at the end of the war. Sweets too were on coupons, though some shopkeepers such as Miss West on the Town Hall corner of Long Street often had some 'under the counter'. Bengers' sweet shop in Bath Road became a mecca for British and American servicemen, though Mrs Benger's famous home made ice cream could not always be produced through shortage of cream and sugar. Airmen often walked in from Melksham to buy sweets and cigarettes, but once when the shop had sold all its goods, only jugs of water could be provided for them.

Petrol was rationed from the beginning of the war, and was only available for business or official purposes, the number of coupons varying with the horsepower of the car. Traffic on the roads was discouraged as much as possible to avoid disrupting military movements, In August 1944 the director of a Chippenham firm was fined for driving to Devizes on business when he could have made the journey by public transport. The use of other fuel was also restricted. The Ministry of Fuel and Power advised that bath water should not exceed 6" in depth. Coal was limited to 2 tons a year per household and in a severe winter many people could be found collecting firewood from fallen trees on Roundway Down. Wessex Electricity suggested heating only one room at a time and that fires should not be switched on until after 1 p.m.; – 'the great war effort must go on, cold or not. So do a few physical jerks and keep that fire off'.

Clothes too were rationed, and women's ingenuity was tested to provide for their growing families, although extra coupons were available for wool to make baby clothes, and for rapidly growing

'Make Do and Mend'

teenagers, provided their height, weight and shoe size were verified by the school. Jackets were 'turned', petticoats were made from old bedspreads, coats from blankets and most women knitted their own stockings. Occasionally silk parachutes, either whole or in sections, could be bought in Devizes market. These were highly prized for the silk was of beautiful quality and was coupon free. The snag was that they were criss crossed with strong seams, so that only small areas of silk could be salvaged, and making a garment was like doing a jigsaw puzzle. If one was very thrifty and even more patient, one could unpick the seams and not only have parachute silk but also a quantity of stout thread as well. The material was soft and hard wearing and much used for small garments, particularly the french knickers so popular at that time among the young. Elastic was in very short supply for knickers so tape was used instead. Very popular were siren suits, all-in-one warm boiler suits to wear in the shelters, but it was difficult to obey the call of nature when zipped up. The shortage of rubber led Clark's, the shoe firm, to make hinged wooden-soled clogs, with rubber or leather stuck on at intervals, though this made them slippery. There were long queues in the Brittox when Sloper's received a supply of cycle batteries, but a practical alternative was a special acetylene light.

It was the age of 'Make Do and Mend'. Everyone was exhorted to save materials for salvage, such as old bills, letters, magazines, string and newspapers; these were to be placed in separate heaps for doorstep collection, or in the bins located around the town which were emptied daily. In January 1942, a record 35 tons 5 cwts of paper were collected in Devizes. Greasy paper, however, was kept for lighting fires and Christmas wrapping paper was supposed to be saved to be re-used. Even rubber screw stoppers from beer bottles were needed for salvage. Bones, too, were saved to make glue and fertilisers and placed in receptacles in various parts of the town, though these were often raided by local dogs. Kitchen waste was set aside for pig food and schoolchildren were encouraged to collect rose hips for making syrup and honey. Fuel watchers in offices, shops, factories and hotels had to see that there was no unnecessary wastage of fuel by switching lights and radiators off, shutting doors and placing firebricks in open fires. Farmers were encouraged to re-use and mend sacks and to save binder twine which was in short supply, and they were given advice on how to economise on tractor fuel. The President of the National Savings Committee set a good and appropriate example when he sent a message to the mayor of Devizes during Wings for Victory Week by carrier pigeon.

An advertisement in the *Devizes Gazette* for 24 June 1943 publicised a Pifco Sharpex Razor Blade Sharpener which could make a blade last a whole year. Water too must be saved because of the pressure on the town's water supplies; vehicles should not be washed or gardens watered. Soap, soap flakes and powder were rationed and Mazo advertised soap energizing tablets to make the washing powder go further. A prominent feature of the National Savings campaign was the 'Squanderbug', who supposedly tempted people to spend on non-essential articles and so prevented them from investing in National Savings. But in fact few consumer durables were available. Only utility furniture was manufactured during the war and points were needed for all except nursery furniture, the replacement of bomb damaged goods or for setting up house. Furniture could only be obtained through a local retailer to save carriage.

The general theme of the war years was 'Save It' and Devizes people learned how to make their own individual contribution to the battle of production by thrift and inventiveness. Whether packing tins of cigarettes to send abroad to British soldiers, collecting scrap metal for the fighter fund, stretching the rations to feed a hungry family or growing cabbages and potatoes, everyone was made to feel part of the war effort. 'Evenings in the factories,' ran the Government advertisement, 'weekends on a farm, hours in the vegetable garden – all these make time well spent in waging the battle of production. This is no time for keeping the wheels merely greased and turning. It is the time when every man and woman in Britain must produce, themselves, all the many and different wheels of war – and victory'.

Squanderbug advertisement in the *Wiltshire Gazette* 7 January 1943

Left hand advertisement reads:-
Beware the treacherous Squander bug! He's the Prince of fifth-columnists–doesn't believe in a nest-egg for the future–doesn't believe in making money fight for Britain. He's all for chucking good money on useless things that don't help to win the war. Don't let him fool *you*. Buy Savings Certificates with all you can spare. Join a Savings Group to defeat the Squander Bug!

Right hand advertisement reads:-
Watch the change you've got left when you've finished the essential shopping or you'll only fritter it away...that's the Squander Bug at work! *He* doesn't want you to have a nest-egg for the future. He *hates* money going to help the war. Squash him–turn that loose change into 6d, 2/6 and 5/- Savings Stamps.–That'll *larn* him!

39

CHAPTER 5

THE COMMUNITY SPIRIT

Another effect of the war was the curtailment of social life due to the blackout, although in many ways the war brought people together for company and comfort. Petrol was short, and journeys to the coast were banned from the Wash to Cornwall, so people were restricted to purely local activities. Evening classes at Devizes Grammar School were popular, with subjects ranging from Drama, Wartime Cookery, French, Shorthand and Bee-Keeping to Woodwork and Folk Dancing. The Philharmonic Choir also continued to function and give concerts, and churches were full, especially when some disaster occurred, such as the loss of a battleship and a cruiser off Singapore. Pat Kennedy recalls chairs being placed in the aisles at the Catholic church to provide enough seats, as the congregation was augmented by evacuees and soldiers' wives.

Many social activities in the town centred round providing entertainment for the troops. At the Garrison Theatre on the London Road, entertainment was provided by E.N.S.A., culminating in the visit of Bob Hope. Once the Catholic padre asked that St Joseph's school choir should sing at a camp service and an American lorry was sent down to fetch them and bring them back. Local busybodies were aghast at seeing the Kennedy girls alighting from an army lorry! The soldiers' room in Commercial Road, run by Miss Blanche Anstie, gave a warm welcome to British soldiers on Wednesday, Saturday and Sunday evenings and provided a quiet room where they could read and write letters, while the American Red Cross ran a social centre on the Green. A group of thirty Devizes ladies, led by Dorothy Chivers, worked afternoon, evening and Sunday shifts feeding American soldiers and running an information desk.

Keeping up civilian as well as military morale was an important

Soldiers billeted on a house in the Nursery, Devizes

Devizes volunteers and American soldiers at the American Red Cross Club on the Green on Mother's Day, 14 May 1944. Dorothy Chivers is third from the left

aspect of the war effort. The focus of most people's attention was 'the wireless'. The demand for up to date information had already boosted the number of wireless licences in Devizes from 484 to 529 in 1939. ITMA and Churchill's broadcasts were especially popular, and many people recollect the playing of the national anthems of the Allies before the 9 o'clock news bulletin every Sunday night. There were long queues at the two cinemas, which often showed patriotic films such as 'Henry V' and 'In Which We Serve' or comforting stories like 'Mrs Miniver'. In the later stages of the war, special programmes were organised in Devizes for 'Holidays at Home' with a variety of social functions. The Devizes Hospital Weeks continued throughout the war years and many of the Savings Weeks provided entertainment, such as military parades, swimming galas, fetes, boxing displays and variety concerts, including popular impersonations of Churchill and Hitler. During Wings for Victory Week in 1943, besides a cricket match and rifle shooting, there was even a baseball game staged by American soldiers in Southbroom Park.

First aid and civil defence work, housing evacuees and enduring shortages were not the only ways in which Devizes helped the war effort. Boy Scouts collected waste paper and young people joined the Army Cadet Force, the Air Training Corps, the Girls Training Corps or the Youth Service Corps, who assisted the army and the civil defence by digging gun emplacements, painting kerbstones white and collecting salvage. Women served in canteens, knitted for the Merchant Navy and collected books for the forces. Men filled sandbags and ran whist drives to raise money for worthy causes, while 'The Devizes Wartime Entertainers' gave concerts for the troops and evacuees and the Red Cross collected food parcels to send to British prisoners of war. The station staff of 35 did sterling work coping with a great increase in freight traffic, carrying tanks, food and military supplies as well as personnel. Farmers made a tremendous contribution to feeding the population, and arable production soared. Local people spent their holidays and weekends doing voluntary work on the farms during the long daylight hours provided by Double Summer Time. Many men followed the advice of the Devizes Gardeners and Allotment Holders

The Community Spirit

I WISH TO MARK, BY THIS PERSONAL MESSAGE, my appreciation of the service you have rendered to your Country in 1939.
In the early days of the War you opened your door to strangers who were in need of shelter, & offered to share your home with them.
I know that to this unselfish task you have sacrificed much of your own comfort, & that it could not have been achieved without the loyal co-operation of all in your household.
By your sympathy you have earned the gratitude of those to whom you have shown hospitality, & by your readiness to serve you have helped the State in a work of great value.

Elizabeth R

Testimonial from Queen Elizabeth II received by Mrs Perry of Devizes

How Devizes Won The War

Inauguration in the Market Place, on Saturday, May 22nd 1943, of "Wings for Victory" week by Air Vice-Marshal C.R. Steele D.F.C. accompanied by The Mayor, Councillor C.W. Pugh and Corporation, and Officers of the United States Forces.

American tanks in Devizes Market Place on 10 June 1944 as part of the 'Salute the Soldier Week' parade. Note the water tank to the left of the Fountain.

All out for the 1943 Harvest

This is the most critical year in our history. Hitler still aims to sink our ships—to starve us out. You are fighting the "Battle of the Fields" to defeat him. Every possible ship that might bring us food must now carry tanks and planes and guns. Every extra acre of tillage crops you can grow in 1943 will help to release ships and bring the day of victory nearer.

★ **THE NATION MUST HAVE BREAD**
— grow all the wheat and barley you possibly can.

★ **THE NATION MUST HAVE POTATOES**
— we can never have too many. They are your country's "iron rations"—an insurance against hunger and defeat.

★ **THE NATION MUST HAVE MILK**
— it is vital for young children. Grow the crops needed to keep your herd in full production, especially next winter.

These crops are vital. To make sure that the Nation gets enough of them we must plough up more grassland and increase the tillage area. Any of your grassland that is not essential to maintain your dairy herd—any seeds area that can go into the tillage pool—must grow these war-winning crops.

Play your part in the food production battle

ISSUED BY THE MINISTRY OF AGRICULTURE AND FISHERIES

Ministry of Agriculture advertisement in the *Wiltshire Gazette* 7 January 1943

---

100 lbs. PERSONAL LUGGAGE

Passengers' Personal Luggage is limited to 100 lbs. (by Government Order).

Address each article clearly, showing your Name and Destination Station.

As a precaution place your Name and Home Address inside each piece of Luggage.

Take special care in labelling Folding Mail-carts, Perambulators, Bicycles, &c.

If you MUST travel— TRAVEL LIGHT

BRITISH RAILWAYS
GWR • LMS   LNER • SR

British Railways advice to 'Travel Light'

WHAT DO I DO . . . to go "all out" for victory?

I SAVE everything I can for my local salvage campaign —paper, metal, bones, food scraps.
I SAVE gas, electricity, coal, paraffin and water.
I SAVE money wherever possible and put it into War Savings.
I SPEND every ounce of energy and every minute I can spare in War-winning work. I help local voluntary organisations and, if I can, I dig for victory.
I KNOW that everyone, including *myself*, can do something.

This space is made available by Wadworth & Co., Ltd.

Government advertisement in the *Wiltshire Gazette* 7 January 1943

Association to 'get all they can out of the soil for the replenishment of the family cupboard'.

During the war, a great deal of money was raised in the town by means of National Savings, inspired by the Government slogan 'Lend to defend the right to be free'. Devizes contributed £259,915 in two days in May 1941 for War Weapons Week and £193,000 in February 1942 to adopt the destroyer HMS *Chelsea*. Wings for Victory Week in May 1943 reached a total of £255,000 to provide 5 bombers and Salute the Soldier Week raised a similar sum the following year to equip and maintain a battalion of the Wiltshire Regiment for six months. Street groups were formed for the National Savings scheme and residents were encouraged to give at least 1*s.* in the £ of their wages. £550 was collected for the Red Cross to buy an ambulance for the forces in June 1940 and flag days were held for Aid to Russia and Aid to China. House and street railings were melted down for scrap, including the Market Cross railings and lamp and even rails round tombstones in St James' churchyard. A weapon from another war, the Crimean Gun, which had stood outside the Town Hall for nearly a century, was also sacrificed to the war effort. In the last year of the war, Devizes people generously provided household articles to help rehouse blitzed families in Battersea.

There was a general feeling that 'We're all in it together'. Financial and personal sacrifices had to be made to achieve victory, such a long time in coming and which in the darkest days of the war seemed such a faraway hope.

CHAPTER 6

VICTORY AT LAST

Although peace in Europe was not officially announced by the Prime Minister until 3 p.m. on 8 May 1945, the 'stupendous news' had leaked out and that day the town was full of flags and bunting, decorating buildings, bicycles, cars and even prams, with the photographs of the King and Queen and the Prime Minister prominently displayed in shop windows. Schools and businesses were closed and church services throughout the town were crowded. At the afternoon and evening services at St John's church, the Prime Minister's message was relayed by loudspeaker. 'The Trumpet Voluntary' and 'Land of Hope and Glory' were played and the packed congregation sang 'Praise my Soul the King of Heaven' and 'Now Thank we all our God'.

The Town Council was much criticised afterwards for not organising any official events, but spontaneous celebrations took place in many parts of the town. Hotels and restaurants put on special Victory suppers, and the pubs were allowed to stay open till 11 p.m., though their limited supplies ran out long before that. Bonfires were lit in some areas, including one on the Green where old farm carts were used to fuel the blaze. A bonfire on Roundway Hill, surmounted by a swastika flag, was erected by the Wiltshire Regiment Band and lit by Lady Roundway. The residents of Sheep Street organised street dancing to a local band, and Bengers provided children with free ice cream. Everywhere thunder flashes and fireworks were being let off. The Crammer was illuminated by flares on the water and the facade of the police headquarters in Bath Road was floodlit.

One of the most joyous aspects of the day was the ringing of the church bells, silent for many years as they had been designated the signal for invasion, although they had been rung in 1942 to celebrate the Allied victory at Alamein and on Christmas Day that year.

The following night, 9 May, there was dancing in the Market Place, and street parties were later organised for children in Caen Hill Gardens and Pans Lane. On 7 June the Services arranged a party in the Town Hall to thank all the volunteers who had run the Services Social Centre for six years and raised £1,100 for service charities. The event closed with an exhilarating Victory march through the hall.

For V-J Day on 15 August 1945 the Town Council was rather more prepared and laid on a comprehensive programme. Children were entertained in the Market Place and later a thousand of them, in two batches of 500, enjoyed a tea party and concert in the Corn Exchange, where the centre piece was a 3cwt. iced Victory cake bearing the flags of the Allies. The flags of the U.S.A., Russia and China hung from the Town Hall balcony, and the fountain and the Market Cross were floodlit and hung with coloured lights. The Wiltshire Regiment Band played for community singing in the Market Place and old age pensioners were entertained to dinner. Later there was dancing in the Corn Exchange and the Drill Hall, and fireworks and a bonfire on the Green where the Japanese flag was burnt and everyone seemed to be decked with red, white and blue ribbons.

Although the post war years were to be marked by austerity, with rationing continuing for some time, there was a deep sense of relief that the war was over. Many local men and women would never tread Wiltshire soil again, but during the next few months 1,200 service personnel did return to Devizes and Roundway parishes to be re-united with their families and to return to some semblance of normality. The years 1939–1945 had, however, left their mark and heralded deep social changes, in the position of women in society and in the determination to build a better social fabric. No one survived the war without being affected by it. Privation had tested ingenuity and adaptability, engendering a spirit of co-operation and mutual help. Many had learnt unaccustomed skills of organisation and leadership, taking responsibilty and being part of a chain of command. Of necessity the price of preserving freedom had involved the restriction of civil liberties and close regulation of people's lives, symbolised by identity cards

Victory at Last

and indoctrination by propaganda. This was a time of slogans – 'Make Do and Mend', 'Careless Talk Costs Lives', 'Dig for Victory' and 'Is Your Journey really Necessary?', a trend reflected in the entertainment world by the catchphrases of programmes like ITMA. But these Government slogans had given people a sense of the use and purpose of everyone's contribution to the war effort and nurtured a spirit of cohesion and community. The popularity of 'Dad's Army' is a testimony to our nostalgia and admiration for a nation, fumbling yet determined, fighting for its belief in freedom.

Lorna Haycock

Devizes Town Council at the end of the war in 1945

Devizes Market Cross floodlit on VJ+1 night, with fairy lights in the trees and fireworks being let off in the Market Place

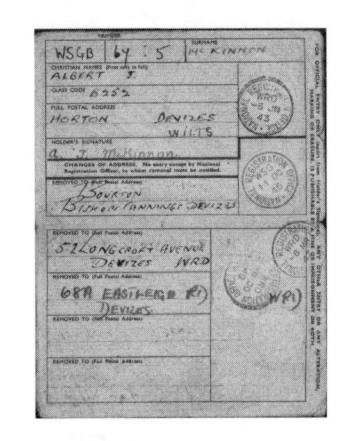

Part II
On The Home Front

On The Home Front

HOW THE WAR EFFORT WAS NEARLY SABOTAGED IN DEVIZES

A daring escape plot which might have compromised the Allied offensive in Europe and had serious effects on the course of the war was discovered in Devizes in 1944. Camp 23 for German prisoners of war had been established in that year in the hutted camp on the London Road formerly used by the militiamen in 1939. The first party of German prisoners arrived after the fighting at Falaise, and thereafter 2,500 came in 5 special trains a day at two hourly intervals; 5 trains departed every day to take them to longer term quarters all over the United Kingdom. Guarding and escorting these prisoners to and from the station was a major exercise and about 1,000 British military policemen were based at the barracks for this purpose. 30 policemen accompanied each group on the train and 30 escorted the prisoners to and from the camp.

The Germans, who were all 'other ranks', were marched four abreast by way of Avon Road, Rotherstone and Commercial Road to avoid the town centre. Most of them looked weary and dispirited in their battle stained uniform or even barefoot and in their underpants. Many were mere boys. When they reached the London Road camp, they were taken to a long hut and stripped, any useful equipment such as leather being put aside. In another room, German doctors inspected them, grading them according to any maladies; some were marked L for lice or S for scabies. After a shower they were given prisoners' clothes, then they were deloused by means of a spray gun pointed up their sleeves and down their trousers. After being fed and bedded down, they were sent off with rations the next day to more permanent quarters.

Later in the war, a longer term base camp was established, consisting at times of as many as 7,000 prisoners, including some trouble makers from other camps. Security was a constant problem and military discipline had to be rigidly enforced. Every morning there was a military parade in each of the 10 compounds; every night the men were counted by the Duty Officer. The Germans were guarded by a company of the Pioneer Corps and a Polish guard company. Naturally there was little love lost between the Poles and the Germans. There were frequent attempts at escape and at least one tunnel was dug. Another group broke out but came back of their own free will. One German got as far as Dover and planned to cross the Channel by motor boat, but ill-advisedly bought some petrol from a British soldier. Wire fences and carbide flares were later installed to foil escape attempts.

Just before Christmas 1944 a group of fanatical Nazis who had recently arrived at Camp 23 hatched a plot to liberate the 7,000 prisoners and then steal armoured vehicles and planes from R.A.F. Yatesbury. They would link up with another group of POWs from a camp in Sheffield and march on London. But the plot was uncovered when two German-speaking Americans visiting the camp overheard the leader, Warrant Officer Erich Palme-Koenig of the Parachute Corps, remark, 'The arms store is the key'. When they reported the incident, hidden microphones were reactivated in the camp, with the result that the British authorities learned the date of the break out. The German plotters were surrounded by British paratroopers armed with sten guns and confined to their huts. The ringleaders were transferred to another POW camp in Perthshire. Koenig and four other conspirators were later found guilty of the murder of a German interpreter whom they had suspected of being an informer, and they were hanged in October 1945.

Lorna Haycock and Mollie Heath

German prisoners of war marching past St James' churchyard on their way to Devizes station in 1944

On The Home Front

AIR RAID PRECAUTIONS

Air raid wardens were recruited at the beginning of the war and included both men and women. Their duties were to get to know their areas of the town and the people living there, to check on the black out and individual fire equipment such as sand buckets for extinguishing incendiary bombs, and stirrup pumps for putting out small fires. In the event of a bombing raid they were responsible for the residents in their area. Devizes was divided into thirteen sectors, each with a sector Head Warden and a deputy. The Head Warden, in charge of all the town's wardens, was Alderman R. Maslen. He was also the head of number 9 sector, which includ-

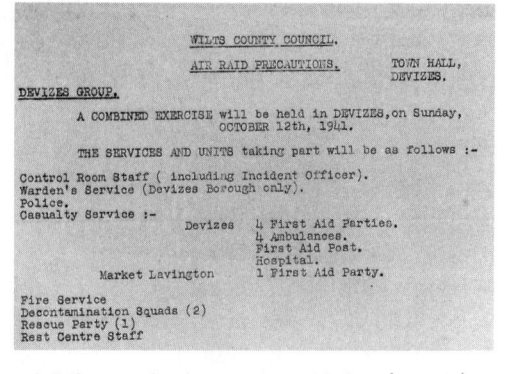

A.R.P. exercise instructions 12 October 1941

ed Mr S. Holley and was based at Mr Maslen's house on the corner of Hare and Hounds Street and Bridewell Street. When Mr Maslen was posted to the headquarters in Trowbridge Mr Coles took over. Wardens, who were unpaid, were on call at all times and had to report to their posts whenever the air raid siren sounded. They were expected to patrol their own areas every evening at dusk to make sure that all was well blacked out.

At the beginning of the war the wardens were not issued with any uniform, but were given a silver badge, with a crown over the letters A.R.P., to wear in their lapels. Later on they were issued with navy blue boiler suits, and eventually navy blue battle dress, originally with silver but later with bone buttons, and a Civil Defence badge sewn on the pocket. All members had to attend a training session each week. These were organised by the police and included first aid, dealing with panic and hysteria and recognition of the various gases which might be used. At one practical session they were sent into a building which was thick with smoke from burning straw bales to learn how to keep low and find their way out again. On another occasion they had to go into a room full of gas, wearing their gas masks but taking them off and making for the exit to prove that the masks really worked. Wardens trained as Incident Officers wore a special badge on their uniform and also a blue covering on their steel helmets. They were trained to set up an incident room near an emergency and had to organise clear routes up wind of any fires so that emergency vehicles could come and go without delay. If there was no suitable room available they had the authority to commandeer a room in a house.

On exercises the wardens worked with other civil defence units and with the police, fire brigade and the ambulance service. One evening on a wardens' exercise, all sectors were told to stay in their posts to await instructions which would be brought round to them. The London Road sector waited and waited but no one came. Finally they gave up and put a notice on the door – 'Direct hit. All dead' and went home. In one combined exercise at Market Lavington, an enemy plane was supposed to have been shot down in the area and the crew had to be captured as soon as possible.

But things did not go as planned. Three boys from Dauntsey's School volunteered to be the Germans and spoke in German all the time. When they demanded the uniform from the first person they met, the local policeman, he told them that he could not give it to them but that he would pretend to be dead and unable to report seeing them. They then proceeded to the exercise headquarters where two of them put up their hands but the third pretended to have a gun and marched them as prisoners towards the base. As soon as they were inside, the front boys stepped aside and the one at the back was able to machine gun all the occupants. The officer in charge commented that it was not really fair as 'you must have a controlled enemy in an exercise'.

During the flying bomb period in 1944, twelve volunteer wardens from Devizes went to Purley in Surrey for two weeks to give the wardens there a rest. On their return each of them received a letter of thanks from Purley and also from the Chief Constable of Wiltshire. After the war several wardens remained in the A.R.P., training for nuclear attack and the hazard of radiation.

Meriall Moore

THE ROLE OF DEVIZES TELEPHONE EXCHANGE

The telephone exchange was situated in St John's Street next to Castle Lane and behind the Post Office. The staff worked in shifts – 8 a.m. to 4 p.m., or 12 noon to 8 p.m. The night shift was 8 p.m. to 8 a.m., and there was also a split shift from 9 a.m. to 1 p.m. and 5 p.m. to 8 p.m. Soldiers with fixed bayonets were on duty outside the exchange at all times and passes had to be shown before anyone was allowed into the building. The night shift was manned by the male members of staff but when they were called up, the girls had to do some night duty with the men. Some of the girls lived in villages, even as far out as Tilshead and they had to cycle to work. Fire watching had to be done from the roof of the exchange. Fire watchers were paid 1s.6d. ($7\frac{1}{2}$p) in summer and 2s.3d. (12p) in winter.

How Devizes Won The War

All telephone calls had to be entered on tickets giving the phone numbers and the length of time taken on each call, the cost being worked out later. Phone calls were cheaper on Christmas Day so the exchange was always very busy as so many of the troops wanted to phone home. After Dunkirk many of the soldiers were sent to Devizes from the ports and this was the first opportunity for them to phone home and to tell their families that they were safe. The telephonists were so busy at this time that they became knee deep in tickets. All subscribers on the Devizes exchange had to be on party lines during the war, including even the doctors and midwives.

Air raid warnings came through to the exchange on a special line.

The codes were :-
	Yellow	Danger coming nearer
	Red	Danger overhead
	Purple	Danger passing away
	White	All clear

The codes were passed on to the local police, the fire brigade and ambulance stations and to nearby towns such as Bath, Melksham and Trowbridge. When the sirens went off at red alert, everyone at the exchange, except the supervisors, had to go to their air raid shelter in the cellar of a private house on the opposite side of Castle Lane. They were not allowed to come out, even to go home, until the all-clear had sounded. Special gas masks were kept at the exchange. These were made of thicker rubber than the civilian ones and had built in earphones and a microphone so that the work of the exchange could continue during raids. They were very hot and stuffy but they had to be worn sometimes for practices. In the areas where bombing was actually taking place, the exchanges were closed down for the duration of the raid. Nearby exchanges were notified and were informed when they reopened if they were undamaged.

Meriall Moore

THE MOBILE MEDICAL SERVICES

On the outbreak of war, in company with a number of people wishing to keep their cars on the road, I volunteered as a driver, oblivious of the fact that I had very little experience (I was ready to take the test when it was suspended for the duration). I was asked if I would instead become an ambulance attendant. There were plenty of vacancies for these, and this is how I became part of the somewhat grandly titled 'Mobile Medical Services'. In Devizes Dr George Waylen directed the medical side and Mr Leonard Trumper was the Transport Officer in overall charge of vehicles. These included ambulances, each manned by a woman driver and attendant, and cars for first aid squads consisting of four men, one being the driver. There were also cars available for slightly injured casualties; it was this service that I hoped to provide. We were required to attend lectures on first aid and gas warfare and to pass examinations in each, and were advised to attend home nursing courses, although a nursing qualification was not compulsory. We were also expected to keep our ambulances scrubbed out and to check that the equipment (stretchers, grey woollen blankets and shiny metal vomit bowls) was ready. The drivers had to see that the ambulances were in good working order and were kept topped up with petrol. We all had to take part in occasional exercises, sometimes in the town but also sometimes on a larger scale in conjunction with other Wiltshire towns. There were infrequent church parades, usually associated with a special occasion, such as Wings for Victory Week, which we were expected to attend.

We were issued with steel helmets, respirators (slightly more complicated than those issued to civilians), a navy drill overall and a navy great-coat, which was so heavy that I could hardly walk in mine. Ambulance attendants also had a black bag, filled with bandages and plasters and a supply of labels, which had to be filled in at the site of any incident and attached to the casualties. Protective clothing for gas was not issued individually but was available at the gas depot. At night we were on a duty rota and

How Devizes Won The War

> DECONTAMINATION OF AMBULANCE.
>
> DECONTAMINATION DEPOT — Lemon Grove, New Park St. Devizes.
> Decontamination Depot Tel: No. — Devizes 384.
>
> 1. All personnel to wear Protective Clothing.
> 2. See that the wash down is wet and bleached.
> 3. Have bleach made up in bin ready, with brushes, buckets, and pump at hand.
> 4. See that all locks at the Depot are fixed.
> 5. When ambulance arrives, the driver and attendants should give a hand before they cleanse themselves, also find out if they have been in contact with Gas, if so, driver's cabin will have to be decontaminated, if not close windows of cab.

Instructions to ambulance drivers

> BRITISH RED CROSS SOCIETY.
>
> Anti-Gas Training Examination.
>
> PLEASE NOTE:
> Candidates should only answer 4 questions.
> Candidates taking the Elementary Examination should answer questions 1, 2a or 2b, 3 and 4.
> Candidates taking the Advanced Examination should answer questions 3, 4, 5 and 6a or 6b.
> Candidates taking the third or subsequent Examinations should answer questions 5, 6a or 6b, 7 and 8.
>
> 1. Does the respirator afford protection against all gases? What are the precautions that are necessary in the storing of a respirator?
>
> 2a. How do you treat eyes affected by mustard gas:-
>   (a) Vapour
>   (b) Liquid.
>
> 2b. What precautions should be taken by those out of doors in a gas contaminated area?

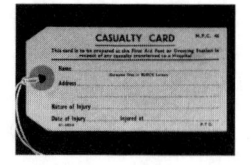

Extract from an anti-gas examination paper for Mobile Medical Service personnel

when the air raid siren sounded we had to report to the bus depot in Station Road and wait until the all clear. It was a cheerless place to spend half the night.

As fortunately there were no notable incidents in Devizes, we had very little to do; in fact the nearest I got to having a casualty in my ambulance was someone my driver knocked down in Devizes Market Place. Luckily he was able to get up and walk away, indignantly refusing our offer of a lift to the hospital for a check up. He told us what we could do with our ambulance and gave us his opinion of women drivers!

There was, however, one occasion when we almost saw active service. On the nights of 25 and 26 April 1942, Bath was blitzed. The two consecutive nights had exhausted the city's own services, and on the third night, fearing yet another raid, they sent for help from other towns in the area. Devizes was asked to supply a first aid team and an ambulance; I went with the ambulance. We reported at the depot at about eight o'clock, and having checked our equipment, went on to what was then called the Public Assistance Institution (later St James' Hospital, now demolished) to collect rations for the night and blankets for our own use. Then off we set, the first aid party in front and the ambulance close behind. It was a lovely April evening, and as we travelled west, I prayed fervently that if the worst happened, I should know what to do and be able to do it.

At Box we stopped, for this was the meeting place for all the vehicles from various other towns and here we formed a long convoy of first aid squad cars, ambulances and rescue and demolition lorries. While we were waiting to go into Bath, lorry loads of people were coming out to spend the night in the fields. We had already passed some families camped out under the trees by the roadside and crowded cars sped by to the safety of the country; one actually had a settee tied to the roof, so someone meant to spend the night in comfort! There was even a hand cart loaded with furniture being trundled by, perhaps all that was left of someone's possessions. Demolition squads, who had been at work all day in Bath, were returning from the city, dirty, tired looking men, covered with dust and grime, very different from the spick and span squads going in with obviously unused picks and shovels.

Eventually, after what seemed a long wait, we began to move off, slowly and with frequent unexplained stops. Every time we ground to a halt, the leader of the first aid party immediately behind us got out and ran to the head of the convoy to see why we had stopped. He came from Trowbridge and was a neat but fussy little man; we were destined to see more of him during the night. I was relieved to find that we were not to go right into Bath, but were to spend the night at Batheaston. If and when we were needed a guide would be sent to show us where to go. There was no bomb damage to be seen this far out of Bath.

We were directed to a little lane, a left hand turning off the main road, which led to the river Avon, although we did not go as far as that. There was some confusion here as vehicles came down the lane and turned to face the main road, ready for any calls that might come. No one seemed to be in charge, so one of our first aid party, who could not resist a bit of organising, took it upon himself to direct the traffic. The result of this, whether by accident or design I cannot say, was that the fussy little man was at the head of the queue at the junction with the main road, while we were well down the lane at the end.

As soon as the parking arrangements were complete, we went off to find the canteen or rest room , but it was so crowded with A.R.P. personnel that we gave up the attempt to get in and went back to our vehicles to see what had been provided for the six of us in the box of rations. We found six tins of corned beef, two loaves of bread, a POUND OF BUTTER!, a large lump of cheese, a tin of treacle, a tin of milk and a tin of cocoa with a label saying that it had been given by kind friends in America. We wondered whether we were meant to stay for a week when we saw all that. If I remember rightly, the butter ration per person per week at that time was 2 ounces. So we settled down to our supper. 'I'll cut the bread,' said our organiser, seizing a loaf (this was in the days before sliced bread), then realising that he had nothing to cut with except the scissors in his first aid kit. I was surprised that none of the men could produce a knife, and offered the penknife I had slipped in my pocket before setting out, thinking that it might come in useful – as indeed it did! Our organiser soon found that it was one thing to sort out a traffic jam, but quite another to cut slices of bread using a penknife with a blade about 2 inches long. The resulting slices consisted of a large hole in the middle with a fringe of bread held together with crust. The tins were of no use to us, as we had no means of opening them (even I hadn't brought a tin opener) but we hacked up the cheese, greedily helped ourselves to the butter and quite enjoyed our al fresco supper.

We had been told that if there was a raid it would probably be either at half past eleven or at half past one, as those were the times the raids had started on the previous nights. At half past eleven the atmosphere became very tense and every time a plane went over even those who were nearly asleep cocked an ear. It was an awful feeling that if the siren sounded it would mean that we were in the target area. In Devizes we had come to believe that the siren indicated that the planes were flying over to some other place. When zero hour passed without incident, we felt that we were safe for another two hours and tried to sleep. As half past one approached, once again we started listening for the throbbing of bomber engines, but all we could hear were the sounds of rushing water from a nearby weir, the soughing of the wind in the burgeoning trees and the braying of a donkey in a nearby field. This zero hour, too, passed without anything happening, but even then we couldn't be sure that there would be no raid. Our organiser had cramp in his leg and went hopping about wildly in the road in the moonlight. His fellows were not a bit sympathetic; they merely remarked what a pity it was that they had not got up to cramp in their first aid course!

Presently there was a disturbance in the form of an ambulance coming down the lane to turn, and there was the little man from Trowbridge fussing again. He plainly wanted an audience. He was terribly thrilled and oozing self importance, because he had had a call! He had been sent with his ambulance to pick up two dead bodies from a house somewhere in Bath. He had gone off to the address he had been given only to find another ambulance on the same errand. He had insisted that it was his call and sent the other ambulance off. The house was locked up, he told us, and he went to great trouble finding who the owner was, knocking him up and obtaining the key. The owner was surprised at being disturbed in the middle of the first quiet night he had had recently, and said that the bodies could stay where they were for the time being, but the little man from Trowbridge insisted on taking them in his ambulance to the mortuary, which also was locked. This time he could not find anyone to unlock it so he set off for the police station, where he collected another body, only to be told by the police to put them back where they were before, so he had his little jaunt all for nothing. It really was a macabre job to have to do in the middle of the night, especially as there seemed no need for it.

It did not get really dark all night, for there was a beautiful moon. We were parked under a plum tree in full blossom, which looked really lovely with the moonlight shining through it. At about half past two, people started coming back from the woods and fields where they had gone for safety, although the first party who rapped at the car window to find out the time seemed uncertain about going on into Bath when they found that it was so early. There were old men, women and children, some of them heavily bandaged.

About a couple of hours later, another of the first aid men was troubled with cramp. He left the car, walked about and then disappeared altogether. Presently he returned, like a ministering angel, with some cups of tea for us. He told us he had gone into the canteen, but found that there was no means of heating the kettle, as the Gas Works had been blown up the night before, and they had run out of oil. Being tall, he had knocked his head against the hurricane lamps hanging from the ceiling, and , being resourceful, he had found some paraffin in these. He said that when he started heating the kettle there were four men in the canteen, all asleep, but by the time the kettle boiled, the place was full, as if by magic. He had poured out tea for us and left the rest for the others. The tea was weak, lukewarm and tasted faintly of paraffin, but in those circumstances and at that hour of the morning, we were not fussy; in fact we were really grateful.

As it began to get lighter, the stars slowly faded and the birds began to sing. Then the third member of the first aid squad woke up to a problem. His was not cramp, but finding himself sitting in a pool of cold water. Apparently he had become so thirsty in the night that he had a drink from the water bottle which the first aid men carried as part of their equipment. He must either have replaced the cork carelessly or dropped off to sleep again before doing so and the remaining water had trickled out on to his seat. He complained that it was all very well for us to laugh but cold water wasn't a bit nice to sit in! He got out of the car and stood with his back to the rising sun to dry off.

We were released just before seven, and had an enjoyable ride home in the spring sunshine. We met people pouring back into Bath after their needless flight into the countryside. Before parting, we shared between us what was left of our rations. And so, about breakfast time, I arrived home, not only unscathed but also the richer by a tin of corned beef and a tin of treacle, and in those days a tin of anything was like manna from heaven!

Olive Chivers

THE W. V. S.

The idea of a women's service to stimulate recruitment into the A.R.P. came to the Dowager Marchioness of Reading while travelling on the Orient Express in the spring of 1938. On her return to England she contacted Sir Samuel Hoare, the Home Secretary, who was very keen to encourage women to help if there was a war. The new Women's Voluntary Service was launched on 18 June 1938, the anniversary of the battle of Waterloo. At first confined to London, it soon spread nationwide and by the end of the year there were 32,329 registered members. All recruits had to sign a form to serve with the A.R.P. or Civil Defence and 'to take any necessary instructions and training and to serve under the direction of officers of the authority concerned'. Administration was carried out by W.V.S. officers but training was supervised by the local authorities. Even the uniforms had to be purchased by the members using their own coupons, though later they were given grants to cover some of their expenses.

Thus the W.V.S. became part of the Civil Defence service and in Devizes they performed a variety of functions. They helped with evacuees or became air raid wardens or billeting officers. Some served as ambulance drivers or offered the use of their cars to drive sitting casualties in an emergency. Many W.V.S. members helped in the canteens for the troops either as cooks or general assistants at the Y.M.C.A. room on the London Road and the Hare and Hounds Street Servicemen's Centre, or in the fully equipped mobile canteen presented by the 'Bundles for Britain' group in the U.S.A.

Older women who felt that they could not commit themselves to active jobs were encouraged to join the 'Housewives Service'. They were allocated to the different sectors into which the town was divided, and were to assist the wardens and get to know the people in their section. In an emergency they would sweep up broken glass, provide hot water, give first aid and generally calm frightened residents and children.

The W.V.S. was responsible for allocating knitting wool for the two knitting guilds in the town and also for individuals knitting for the forces who had to be registered with an official guild or be able to quote the name and number of a related soldier before getting any supplies. They also made regular street collections for National Savings, collected salvage and helped with a clothing store. They were always available for any extra jobs that needed doing in the town, either with the evacuees or the forces. Such voluntary work often gave women organisational skills and a new sense of confidence outside the home. After the war the W.V.S. was able to draw on this wartime experience to continue to fulfil a useful role in the community.

Meriall Moore

On The Home Front

THE WOMEN'S LAND ARMY

By February 1940, there were 170 Land Army girls working in Wiltshire. When girls joined the Land Army, they were sent on a four week training course. As some of the girls were from cities and knew very little about work on the land, they found it very hard and strange. Dauntsey's School in Lavington was at this time an agriculturally biassed school and had its own farm, which the Land Army girls were able to use for their practical training, looking after sheep, pigs and poultry and learning to plough, milk cows and drive tractors. An extra, short course was available to teach hand milking as well as machine milking for any girls going to a farm where it might be needed.

The Land Army uniform consisted of cream aertex shirts, a green pullover and corduroy breeches. The girls were also issued with a khaki hat, long khaki socks and fawn dungarees as well as a pair of brogues and wellington boots. The hours on a farm were long and the work hard for girls not used to country life. Some of the local farms still had horses which had to be rubbed down after work and fed, in addition to being harnessed in the morning. Most farms had at least one tractor which the girls had to drive.

Some of the girls lived in the farmhouse where they worked and some were billeted in private houses or put into hostels. The nearest hostel to Devizes was the one at Potterne erected in April 1942. The hostel girls were taken out to help on farms, private estates or market gardens which needed extra hands at busy times.

There was plenty of entertainment after work. Devizes had two cinemas and the films were changed on Wednesdays and Saturdays. The cost of admission was 1*s.* 6*d.* (8p) for the best seats and 9*d.* for the cheapest. The Land girls often had invitations to the dances and concerts at the barracks. During one Army week in Devizes, a group of them were driven into town by tractor to take part.

As the farm workers were demobilised and came back to work on the farms, the Land Army was slowly disbanded.

Meriall Moore

How Devizes Won The War

Women's Land Army plaque on the Corn Exchange, Devizes

Land girls from Rowde – the Davis sisters, who worked on a farm in London Road, Devizes

Some wartime Devizes cinema programmes

On The Home Front

THE ESTCOURT STREET POST OFFICE DURING THE WAR

During the war, Margaret Henley (neé Kennedy) worked at the Estcourt Street Post Office. Now occupied by Rose's, this sub Post Office, near to the military camps, was a busy place, dealing with married allowances and the dispatch of mail to Service personnel. Parcels sent to the Forces had to be no bigger than a certain size. One woman from Etchilhampton walked to Devizes carrying a huge parcel about four feet long, which was far too heavy and bulky. Three times she had to undo the parcel and pull out innumerable cushions in order to reduce it to the requisite size. After Dunkirk, each soldier was allowed to send one free letter home to inform his family that he was safe. A bedraggled Scotsman appeared to post his letter, with his kilt still hanging in bunches, where he had waded into the sea to the rescue boats. Many wives came to join their husbands who were based in Devizes. When they collected their weekly allowance of £2.7s.6d. on Mondays, their allowance books had to be stamped with a red W for wife. One woman was greatly aggrieved that by some oversight her book had not been stamped and considered it a slur on her character – 'a public slight'.

Lorna Haycock

WAR WEAPONS WEEK AND OTHER FUND RAISING EFFORTS

(Taken from a letter to a pen friend in South Africa, dated 9 June 1941)

'The last week in May was our local War Weapons Week. We hoped to raise a total of £100,000 during the week by sales of National Savings Certificates, War Bonds, Defence Bonds and deposits in Post Office Savings Banks etc. On the opening day, Empire Day, we had a very 'high up' Army Officer to open the day, and he and the Mayor in his traditional gold chain were on a platform erected in the Market Place. There was a grand procession around the town, consisting of all the fire engines from the town and district, the Air Raid Wardens, the Demolition Squads, First Aid Parties, Ambulances, Red Cross Nurses, Women's Voluntary Service, Women's Land Army, a contingent of munition workers and contingents from the Army, the Navy, the Air Force and the A.T.S., and I don't know how many military bands. It was very impressive – a choir of children from all the town schools sang 'Land of Hope and Glory' and other songs, and the children of one of the private schools gave a patriotic tableau. Members of Guides and Scouts were also present. Various speeches were made and the War Weapons Week was declared open. The total on the first day was £82,000 so we felt very pleased with ourselves. The total at the end of the week was the magnificent one of £259,915, so that we more than doubled our objective. The Grammar School raised £625, which was the highest school total. The poor school children have a time of it collecting for one thing or another now. There is the 'Penny A Week Red Cross Fund', then we had a special collection for the Spitfire Fund, and one for a YMCA hut for the soldiers, then one for cigarettes for the troops, and so it goes on. We have now adopted a ship. I don't know what its name is, but it is an oil tanker of the Free French Forces. An oil tanker doesn't sound very exciting, but as they pointed out in a letter to the school, it is bringing a very precious commodity to our shores. They have suggested that some of the children might like to write in French to the French-born members of the crew. I wonder if any of them will.'

An article in the Grammar School magazine of December 1944, headed 'Our Ships' refers to the fact that the school had for over three years been writing and sending parcels to two ships in the Merchant Navy, which had been adopted by the school. In 1945, through its War Charity Fund, the school adopted several Old Boys who were prisoners of war and sent them books, as well as supporting orphans from the Belsen camp.

Olive Chivers

Part III
Reminiscences of The War

How Devizes Won The War

DEVIZES GRAMMAR SCHOOL AT WAR

The school buildings, both the Bath Road building and Braeside, were used as one of the reception centres for evacuees during the war. Evacuation started just before the outbreak of war and when I arrived back from holiday on 2 September 1939, things were in full swing. The first batch of evacuees arrived at Braeside unexpectedly on the Saturday afternoon. Instead of the expected schoolchildren, these were a group of blind adults. Their leaders were very put out to find that they were not expected. It must have been very distressing for the blind, but we did the best we could for them, putting up camp beds, giving them tea and leading them from room to room. Evidently the mistake was put right, for by the next morning they had moved off to some other destination.

On Sunday 3 September, the school hall at Bath Road was astir with activity. A train load of schoolchildren was expected and little brown carrier bags were being filled with rations to last a day or two for each child. At eleven o' clock, we heard on the radio of the declaration of war, stood to attention for the National Anthem and then got on with whatever we were doing, wondering what the future would hold for us all. When a little later the evacuees arrived, they were not schoolchildren but mothers and babies. The Billeting Officers had the job of taking these to people who were expecting children. Many of them did not stay long once it was apparent that the expected air raids on London were not happening. The women were appalled to find that they had to walk from street to street; they were accustomed to going everywhere by bus.

In September 1940, at the height of the invasion scare, another batch of evacuees arrived, this time from Hastings, comprising families and some elderly men. In a letter to a friend dated 23 September I wrote, 'It was very dark before the train arrived, and the evacuees were divided into three groups, and one group of about 180 men, women and children came to our school for the night. We gave them tea and sandwiches and issued army blankets for them to sleep on. Most of them were so grateful for all we could do for them, even though they had to sleep on the floor. About half of them slept in the main school building and the rest

Reminiscences of the War

at Braeside. They were all settled down by about half past ten. Two mistresses and one master were on duty in each building. At Braeside the Senior Mistress went round trying to reassure the nervous ones (some of them were in a very bad state of nerves, as they had had very little sleep for weeks). At first they wanted to know where they were, as they thought they were going to Somerset. So the Senior Mistress said, 'You're in Devizes, in the middle of Wiltshire about thirty miles from Bristol' – when she was drowned by an hysterical wail of 'The Bristol Channel area! That's what they go for!' Then someone remarked on the number of planes about, and the Senior Mistress further put her foot in it by saying, 'Oh yes, they're trainers. We have a lot of aerodromes in Wiltshire'. That innocent remark was greeted by another agonised yell of 'Aerodromes? Oh that's what they're trying to get!' So the Senior Mistress said, not very convincingly, 'Yes, they do the aerodromes round the coast, but not Wiltshire ones'. Then someone else started worrying about the German panes which passed over here, quite harmlessly as a rule, every night. The Senior Mistress tried to persuade them that they were our planes and heard them remark behind her back, 'She doesn't know a Jerry when she hears one!'.

I turned up at 7.30 the next morning to help with the breakfast. By that time some of the evacuees had found a brush and swept up their room, and were ready to help with the washing up. After breakfast the Billeting Officer started trying to billet them. This was a slow job as the town was very full and it was difficult to billet whole families who refused to be split up. By lunch time, about sixty were still left, so they were all taken to Braeside, where the school cook managed to provide a meal for them in the confined space of the Braeside kitchen. During the afternoon a mistress from the Ursuline High School and I held the fort, providing tea for twenty people who were left over and innumerable cups of tea for the poor exhausted Billeting Officers. The last lot of evacuees, a family of six, were billeted about half past seven, and we then sat around for a final cup of tea and had a good laugh about all the funny things that had happened.

Olive Chivers

How Devizes Won The War

DEVIZES GRAMMAR SCHOOL WARTIME ACTIVITIES

During 1942 and 1943 fire watching was in operation at the Bath Road building. Braeside was exempt as there was a caretaker living on the premises. Three members of staff or older pupils were on duty each night and camp beds were provided. Fire watchers were paid 3s. a night during the summer months and 4s. 6d. during the winter. If the siren sounded, they were to look for incendiary bombs with the stirrup pump at the ready.

For several years, the school ran harvest camps during the summer holidays at Higher Bridmore Farm in south Wiltshire, where work was done on several farms. Each camp lasted a month and on average there were about forty children at any one time. The work included stooking, carting, ricking and threshing. A ten hour day was worked and a great deal of fun was enjoyed at the same time.

Olive Chivers

MEMORIES OF A DEVIZES GRAMMAR SCHOOL WARTIME PUPIL

When a new school year commenced a week after war was declared, we found that we were sharing the school with the Ursuline Convent School from London and a part-time sharing system was started. Most classes also had a few extra children who had come to stay with relatives for the duration of the war. Gas masks had to be taken to school every day and there was regular gas mask drill. Sometimes gas masks were worn for part of a lesson. Later when an extra filter was added, the elongated masks got in the way of our books. To prepare for the eventuality of incendiary bombs, we enjoyed stirrup pump practice, with water spraying everywhere. We also practised passing buckets of water in a chain. Strips of gauze were stuck crossways on windows to reduce the risk of glass shattering in a raid. When the air raid siren went, we lined up in a passage way at Braeside. On one occasion we went down Little Lane during a raid and later the cellars were opened up.

Reminiscences of the War

Buses were scarce so in the early part of the war there often wasn't a bus to take us home at the end of the school day. The junior forms went home earlier than usual and the seniors had to wait until 5 o'clock for a bus, so we used to gather round a piano and sing the latest popular songs, such as 'Run,Rabbit, Run' and 'We're going to hang out the Washing on the Siegfried Line'. For a few days after Dunkirk, there were no buses at all to take us home and we had to walk. One day some children had a lift for part of the way sitting on crates of jam; others had a lift in a furniture van.

The school was very short of exercise books, so every page had to be completely filled and sometimes we had to use loose paper. Swimming lessons were cancelled because the pool was needed for the armed forces. In the autumn we had to collect hips to provide vitamin C for babies aand small children. Some pupils left school at 14 to work on their family farms.

In spite of the wartime conditions and many masters being called up, we were still expected to work hard and pass the School Certificate.

Dora Seymour

'LOOK, DUCK AND VANISH'

In May 1940, with the threat of invasion hanging over us, a new force was set up, the Local Defence Volunteers, to man observation posts and set up road blocks. I was then 17 and eagerly went to register at the police station. At the first meeting held at the Scout Hall, we discovered that most of the recruits were veterans from the Great War. We were sworn in and issued with our 'uniform', a black armband with the letters LDV, or as some wags dubbed it 'Look, Duck and Vanish'. I was put into number 1 Platoon and our post was in the old summerhouse at the back of Rotherstone allotments.

We had a fearsome collection of weapons – 12 bore shot guns, .22 rifles, and .45 revolvers. I managed to acquire a Winchester .45 rifle and ammunition from a retired gamekeeper. It had a kick like a mule. In the evenings we did shooting practice, firing air rifles at tins. Some men even had kitchen knives which were ground down until they were razor sharp.

Soon the LDV became the Home Guard. We were given our uniform with the badge of the Wiltshire Regiment and issued with American P17.300 rifles. We now practised on proper rifle ranges but somehow the early magic had gone.

Arthur Cleverly

WITH THE A.T.S. IN DEVIZES

As a member of the A.T.S. (now W.R.A.C.), I was sent in 1941 to the artillery radar training school at Devizes barracks, on the site of the present London Road industrial estate. It was a very intensive two months course and we had very little free time in which to leave the camp; in fact I remember being able to get into Devizes only twice, both times after dark in the blackout, so I have very few visual memories of that time. I do, however, remember vividly a wonderful canteen run by local volunteers. I often wonder whether those generous hearted ladies ever realised what it meant to us to know there was somewhere warm and welcoming to visit outside the camp. Despite food rationing, there was always something to eat, plentiful hot and cold drinks and unlimited smiles for soldiers and airmen.

My strongest memory of those times is of being drilled by a drill-sergeant of the Coldstream Guards. He had never trained girls before and considered the job very much beneath his dignity. Also, I believe, he was being teased by his fellow sergeants in the mess, because he greeted us on our first day with 'I don't intend being made a laughing stock by a bunch of —— girls, so watch it!' He reduced some of the girls to tears and we all got blisters, but before long we found ourselves enjoying it, and at the end of the course the sergeant had the grace to say he had never had a squad of men who had learned more quickly or become smarter than we had, and he was proud of us.

Reminiscences of the War

Devizes barracks and military hospital

The flax factory, London Road, Devizes, which was set up in 1940, processed locally grown flax into fibres to make webbing for parachute harnesses

I have had the pleasure of living in Devizes for the past seventeen years, but I am afraid my memories of Devizes in war time are only of a fierce drill sergeant on the barracks square and of the warm welcome extended to strangers by the kind people of the town.

Pauline Parker

THE BUTCHER, THE BAKER ...

During the first year of the war I was in my last year at the Grammar School in the second year Sixth. After that I was away, at college for three years and then teaching in London. We sixth formers were asked to help with various war preparations, first in the summer holidays of '38 with assembling gas masks in the Corn Exchange, and then in the summer of '39 with arrangements for receiving London evacuees. I can remember being in the school hall, now part of St Peter's School, on the Sunday morning, 3 September, when war broke out. One of the staff turned on a wireless and we all listened to Mr Chamberlain's speech; we youngsters were awed but secretly rather excited, though the older teachers who could remember the first war looked worried and sad.

The first wave of evacuees included families, mothers coming with their children, and so, to keep them together, empty houses were requisitioned for them. My mother was one of the W.V.S. ladies who begged furniture, bedding, kitchen equipment and provisions, and fitted up the houses as well as they were able, but inevitably conditions were a bit spartan.

We had air raid alerts when German planes were going over to Bristol, but in the whole war our area only received the odd bomb here and there, probably off loaded on the way home. I remember one incident when a party of my sisters, brother and cousins were having a picnic on Roundway on Oliver's Castle. We had spread a big white cloth on the grass and were eating our tea when we heard the sirens in Devizes, and then the sound of planes. We hastily gathered up the cloth in case the raiders should see it and flattened ourselves on the steep side of the hill – as if they would be interested in us! We found the episode more impressive and exciting than frightening.

During the war there was a flax factory on London Road on what is now the trading estate on the town side of Folly Road. The flax was stripped from the stalks, bundled and then sent to another factory to be made into webbing. Many local girls, including Mary Townsend and Vera Waller, were directed into working there. Joyce Kemp worked at Devizes Hospital. She was interviewed for war work in an office set up in *The Lamb Inn*, and because she had belonged to the Red Cross she was directed into the Civil Nursing Reserve. These nurses were not given any further training, but had to learn as they went and cope as best they could. They worked long hours, were always short staffed and were subject to many rules and regulations. When tired at the end of night duty they still had to queue up to ask Matron for two nights off. Nevertheless there was a very good spirit during the war and people did not complain.

Joyce, who wore Red Cross uniform at the Hospital, also had to do fire guard duty and her post was at the swimming pool where there was a first aid station. It was not very comfortable sitting in the changing rooms with the blackout in place, because the walls ran with condensation. After one night she and her companions were on the carpet because there had been complaints from neighbours of a raucous party during the night. It was later found that some soldiers had climbed over the wall and disported themselves in the pool.

The Nurses' Home block at the hospital was used to house military patients. Joyce remembers that one day they had to deal with a lot of Home Guard men who had been on a course when a phosphorus bomb had exploded and covered them with glowing fragments. The Home Guard often had exercises in the town and during one in New Park Street a local doctor, who shall be nameless, jammed on his gas mask so quickly that he forgot he had his pipe in his mouth and broke his teeth. Later in the war, Joyce was moved to the Isolation Hospital to do T.B. nursing. These patients needed the windows to be open all the time, so the blackout could not be used, and the nurses crept about their duties with torches.

After Dunkirk, thousands of men were sent here. I heard it said that we had 35,000 troops for a while, and although the camps at Devizes were extensive, they could not cope with the number and men were sleeping on the ground. They arrived ragged, partially clothed and exhausted. Some of them wandered about the town or sat on the pavements, and soon a canteen was opened for them in the Shambles. Joyce can remember an officer coming to her door in Potterne Road asking for water for their truck. Her father invited in the truck load of men and plied them with sherry.

Leonard Strong says that the influx of troops greatly helped trade in the town and made it a livelier and more prosperous place. When war started Leonard was helping his father to run the family bakery and restaurant, first in The Brittox and then from 1940 at 35, the Market Place, when he took over sole running of the business. He borrowed £100 from his cousin, to buy a carpet for the restaurant, and 6 Lloyd Loom tables and 24 chairs – and they are still there to this day! The business took off immediately and the restaurant was full for two sittings. The ration allowances were made according to the number of customers served, and Strong's meat allowance was 30*s.* a week. With this Leonard bought three legs of lamb at 7*s.*6*d.* each and 7*s.*6*d.* worth of shin and kidney for steak and kidney pies. Fish was available from Mr Batt in the Little Brittox, and there was powdered egg for omelettes. Leonard recalls that the restaurant trade was boosted by all the troops including Canadians, Americans and American nurses and he remembers them all as being very pleasant and well behaved. There were sometimes Wings for Victory processions in the town, with all the available military taking part to encourage people to buy bonds to help the war effort. Besides the German prisoners of war at the London Road camp, a few Italian prisoners lodged in the castle which Mrs Reed had vacated.

Jack Wishart ran his butcher's shop in Devizes throughout the war in partnership with Bob Cook as Cook and Wishart, though each kept his own shop, Wishart's in the Brittox and Cook's in High Street. Jack was made Meat Allocator for Devizes and the surrounding villages and allocated meat to each butcher and restaurant and organizations such as Roundway Hospital. The meat came in bulk; each butcher had a permit and Jack tried to be fair in giving each one some good meat and some of the rough stuff. He never knew what was coming and there was one difficult week when the entire batch was lambs' hearts, which caused a few grumbles. More than once Jack ran out of meat for his own customers and sold his own ration to keep the peace. At its lowest point, the weekly ration was 8*d.* (4p) worth of meat and 2*d.* (1p) worth of corned beef; the greaseproof paper cost more than the corned beef! Sausages and offal were not rationed and could be sold to non-registered customers when available. Sometimes rabbits were to be had, but some farmers who had thousands of rabbits on their land sold them to London hotels for higher prices. Jack had rabbits offered to him at 6*s.*6*d.* a pound when the official price was 1*s.* a pound.

Archie Hodge, the Town Clerk, was the Food Controller here, Ted Joliffe was the manager at the Food Office and the meat depot was a shed at the back of *The Old Crown* in New Park Street. There were plenty of officials, with petrol allowances for their cars to oversee all the arrangements – Jack used to say that the officials taught Mr Wishart to swear! On one occasion an officer from the camp brought a group of A.T.S. girl cooks to Jack's shop to learn about joints of meat and how to cut them. One fainted when Jack dug out a sheep's eyes.

Jack was one of the original members of the Home Guard, joining at the Assize Courts. Mr Weaver, a leading light in the musical life of the town, was their Captain. They had night time road patrols and manouevres once a month. One night in 1940 they were called out at 3 a.m. and remained on duty all night because there was a rumour of an enemy landing in Dorset. Jack was eventually transferred to the Intelligence Section of the Home Guard, whose head was Sam Cookman, with the headquarters at Captain Brassey's house at Worton.

There was an observation post on the roof of Ansties' offices in the Market Place. One of the men doing duty there, Mr Underwood, the manager of Morton's shoe shop, suffered frostbite

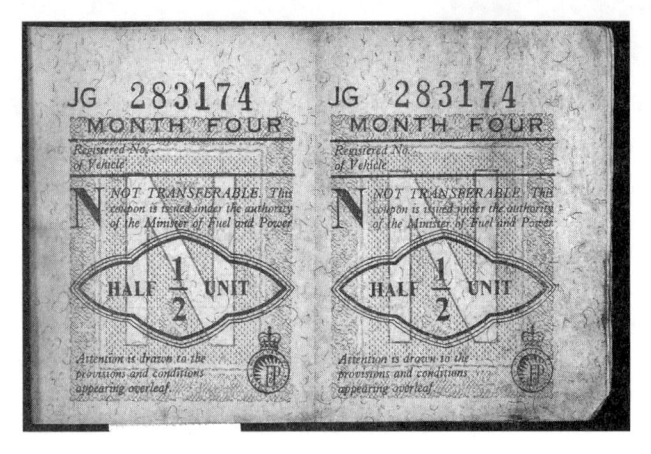

Petrol coupons

Volunteers who ran the Servicemen's Social Club

Back Row Eric May	Mr. Wiltshire (Manager of a dry-cleaners in the Brittox)	Mr. Prior (Manager of Simpson's grocers in Mkt. Place)	Mr. Haines	Don May	?	Mr. James (Congregational Minister)	?		
Middle Row Mr. W.F. Alexander	Mrs. Wiltshire	Mrs. M.R. Rendall	Mrs. Stafford (Midland Bank)	Mr. Yeo	Mrs. Wells	Mrs. Budd	Mrs. Beedell (wife of Manager of LLoyds Bank)	Mrs. Prior	?
Front Row Mrs. Picker (Wife of Barclay's Bank manager)	Mrs. Majorie Ferris	Mrs. Coles	Mr. Wells (Manager N.P.Bank)	Mr. Leon V. Burn (Jeweller, Mkt.Place)	Mr. Coles (Hairdresser chiropodist St. John's St.)	Mrs. James	?		

Reminiscences of the War

and eventually lost a leg. John Bishop acted as errand boy for this post.

Devizes was a busy place during the war with so many troops, among them Americans and Canadians who were made very welcome and who in turn were very generous to the locals. Ladies of the W.V.S. organized the Services' Social Centre in a house which then stood on the corner of Sheep Street and Hare and Hounds Street. They ran a very popular and lively canteen, organizing themselves into teams, each with a leader and each working a whole week in turn. My mother was one of these leaders, and, with this and working at the Y.M.C.A. at the camp, had quite a busy war. Behind the house were extensive work premises which became a concert hall with stage, where there were frequent entertainments. One of the highlights was the visit of Jessie Matthews. Mother was delegated to look after her, taking her home for a meal and helping her in the wings. Jessie was a very highly strung person and requested a chamber pot to be at the ready behind the scenes.

Devizes Cricket Club moved to its present ground in London Road during the war. They were offered the land by Lord Roundway for £1,000 and members, who included Jack Wishart, Charlie Austridge, Joey Weeks, Bob Cook and Phil Ryall worked hard to raise the money, feeling that they were doing it for the men who would come home when peace came. Their main money-raising effort was running hops at the T.A. Hall, which were well patronised as there were plenty of troops here. The army borrowed the ground and maintained it, led by Captain Jellet. He stayed in Devizes after army service and ran *The Cross Keys* in Rowde.

Margaret Worth

How Devizes Won The War

WARTIME CHILDHOOD

Janet Preen

In May 1944, our house in south London was badly damaged in a 'doodlebug' attack. After two weeks in a rest centre, my father, a senior civil servant at the Admiralty, saw an advertisement for a cottage to rent at Wilsford near Devizes, and moved my grandmother, my mother, my brother and myself down in a taxi. It was a thatched cottage opposite the church, with two bedrooms upstairs and one room and a scullery downstairs. There was an enormous fireplace in the living room and we burned anything we could get hold of. At the end of the garden, there was an outside lavatory, and father, who came down at weekends if he could, dug a big hole under a Victoria plum tree to bury the muck. We shared the well in the next door neighbour's garden, until it dried up and all we got out was a bucket of earwigs. Then we had to get our water from the farm down the road. There was no bath or wash basin, and we used to wash in a bucket until father got hold of a canvas basin on a frame. At least we had electricity.

When it rained, the earwigs fell out of the thatch, and our beds were covered with them. I thought that was just as bad as the doodlebugs. One night there was a terrible storm. The water ran down the back path, under the scullery door and into the living room. Next morning when mother opened the door at the bottom of the stairs, she stepped into about a foot of water. She opened the front door and most of it rushed out, but we had to brush out the rest. There was mud all over the floor and the carpet was wringing wet.

The local people were very kind, and we often found bags of vegetables hanging on our door knob. Once there was even a rabbit, shot in a harvest field. Father brought a single electric ring on his second visit from London. We had a big earthenware crock pot which we used for casseroles cooked over the fire, and mother used to bake bread. I remember scrambled dried egg, and sausages which tasted of bread. The church was decorated for the harvest festival, and when the village fete was held in a big marquee on the farm, we took home-made cakes and bunches of sweet peas from the garden.

There was a village shop with a little post office counter. When we were good, mother used to buy us each a bar of Cadbury's Blended Chocolate or Fry's Peppermint Cream. Her own favourite was Victory V Lozenges. On Thursdays we walked to the bus stop (it seemed a long way) and caught the only bus of the week to Devizes. Our weekly treat was home-made marshmallow biscuits in 'The Rendez-Vous' cafe in the Brittox (where Haines and Smith is now). When father came to visit, he used to get the train to Pewsey and then walk to the village. We would walk half way to meet him.

The village was very quiet, with the only noise coming from the American planes. I knew the planes were friendly, so I was never frightened of them. Father called them 'Black Widows', but I never understood why. We did not see any servicemen in the village. We had a radio at the cottage and used to listen to ITMA and Children's Hour. We watched the farm animals being born, and I used to go fishing with my little brother in the mill stream.

Mother was very good at 'make do and mend'. She made me a bathing costume out of an old jumper. She cut the sleeves off and bound the armholes, then she cut off the bottom half and turned it into pants with elastic and more binding. In London we took our gas masks with us everywhere, but in the village we never carried them. I don't remember the village children at all; perhaps they were busy working on the farms. We went back to London at the end of the summer, so I didn't go to school in the village.

D.J. Hair

I went to Southbroom School. We had to take our gas masks every day. We used to hear the German planes going over. The sirens went off and we had to go into the shelters but the bombs did not fall here. Most houses did not have air raid shelters. The air raid wardens came round every night to make sure the blackout curtains were not showing any light. We used army blankets for blackout material. All the cars and lorries had masks on their head-

How Devizes Won The War

Children playing in a sandbagged machine gun post on the Little Green

How to put on a gas mask

lights, even army lorries. There were several static water tanks for putting out fires; one was in Nursteed Road where SCATS now is.

Even though we were rationed, we did not do badly. You could get cracked eggs without coupons and we got bones from the butcher. Father kept greyhounds and used to catch rabbits. We had an allotment too. Clothes were passed down from one child to the next, and even the girls had to wear boys' boots to school.

We used to go on Sunday School outings, paying so much a week. My brother was a 'Bevin Boy', working down the mines. He used to come home on a platform ticket but he never got caught. Father cycled to work at the RAF place at Melksham. He hated the American soldiers, saying that they had too much money and were big headed and always getting into fights.

P.E. Austridge

Flax was grown on land on the London Road during the war and the land girls used to harvest it for the sacking factory. There was a bacon factory in Bath Road and a radio transformer and speaker factory in Pans Lane. In Bridewell Street there was a factory making armaments.

My father had a reserved occupation, managing a shop in Devizes. We had an allotment where Waiblingen Way is now where we grew all our own vegetables. Boys were taught gardening at school so that they could help on the allotments. There were waste food bins on every street. We also had Salvage Weeks, for example for aluminium and paper. When the railings were collected for the war effort, even those outside the Assize Courts were taken. They were cut off with oxy-acetylene jets, which left nasty jagged edges, There were also National Savings drives with targets set for each school.

I went to St. Peter's School. The headmaster, Mr Greed, (or 'Gaffer' as he was known) used to show the children where the war was being fought and go through the progress of the battles with us, using war maps on the classroom walls. We had war maps at home too, cut out of the newspapers.

We all had gas masks in cardboard boxes, which we took everywhere and used to practise with every week at school. All the soldiers had service respirators. Babies had ones like big bags, which they were put right inside. When they got a bit bigger, they had 'Mickey Mouse' gas masks. There were some evacuees at our school, and a girls' school from London was in the Grammar School buildings in Bath Road.

The pubs were all rationed. They got so much beer a week and when it ran out they just shut, but the regulars used to go round the back! Petrol was rationed too. Commercial fuel was coloured and there were severe penalties for anyone who was found with it in his car. There was a sort of 'petrol substitute' made out of petrol and paraffin and Redex which was all right for motorbikes. Petrol lorries were all painted grey, not in the company colours. Some cars were modified to run on gas with big gas bags on their roof. We had to be very careful of our clothes because of the rationing, though there were forged coupons about. There were never enough sweets for the children and no ice cream at all. It was a real treat to be given sweets by the Americans. The boys used to collect chewing gum wrappers and swap them, just like cigarette cards. The American soldiers had big cartons of cigarettes to give away as well.

We occasionally had a day out by train; the furthest we went was Bath. There were scout camps at Erlestoke and Bath, where we went by lorry. There wasn't much evening entertainment apart from the two cinemas and the pubs. There was a garrison theatre with an ENSA unit and people like Bob Hope came to entertain the troops. A lot of the Home Guard used to wangle their way in. The WVS, who were mostly officers' wives and vicars' wives, went round the camps with tea and doughnuts. Cadbury's had a bus, driven by women from Bournville who served cocoa and buns.

We had an air raid shelter in our garden though there wasn't one at school, but there were few air raids. Two bombs were dropped in Marsh Lane and one in Potterne, but they were probably strays. In 1943 when the daylight raids began, we used to see the planes going over in the morning and coming back in the afternoon, some damaged of course. We watched the bombing of Bath from

Prison Bridge – the whole sky was glowing. There were lots of searchlights around but none in Devizes. One large plane crashed in Marsh Lane during school hours, so as soon as we were finished we all ran to see what had happened. We used to see the Paras practising jumping too.

The American soldiers would get a bit over enthusiastic in their training and fire live rounds over public roads. Some of them drove a jeep up Silbury Hill. General Patten came to see them once. The men all disappeared just before D-Day and we wondered where they had gone. The planes for D-Day were hidden all over the place. There was one behind a false wall in a workshop on Caen Hill. I remember when one of our neighbours returned wounded. He was a tall man and he seemed to have got very thin.

The Home Guard used to train on Wednesday evenings and there was also weekend training for them and for the firemen who were also under military discipline. The Observer Corps was based on the corner of a building next to Snuff Street where the railings still exist. There were static water tanks in the Market Place and on the Green and at Avon Road, with chicken wire over the tops to prevent drowning accidents. There were stirrup pumps and buckets of sand in all public buildings.

Marianne Baker

I was born in 1939. My earliest memory is of going to the pictures every Thursday night, from the age of three , and watching the Pathé News. I particularly remember the pictures of Churchill and how everybody cheered when the sinking of the *Bismarck* was shown. One night after the pictures, mother came across five RAF lads who had missed the bus to Upavon so she took them home. They slept on the sitting room floor, then went off very early the next morning to try and hitch a lift back to camp.

We lived in Potterne Wick. When I started school I was taken by single decker bus into Devizes with the other children from Potterne who went to St Joseph's School. Sometimes, going home on market days, the bus was so full that I couldn't reach the bell and missed my stop. There were often a lot of Americans on it going to Tilshead. They seemed gigantic, particularly the black ones. They always had chocolate, gum and small coins in their pockets, which they gave to the children. The child's fare was one penny from Potterne to Devizes, so sometimes I used to buy a penny roll from Strong's in the Brittox and walk home. Surprisingly I never remember having a gas mask.

Our house had four bedrooms, so we often had people boarded on us. There was an old couple, Ben and Jessie Bragg. He had an artificial leg and she used to read the tea leaves in the cup. We also had a brother and sister from London who had been bombed out and who came to school with me. At first they were petrified of country life, particularly the cows, but soon they were enjoying the freedom of playing in the woods. After they went we had some land girls, the overflow from the hostel at Potterne quite close by, They used to go to dances in the village with the Americans. One American, called Don, got back to camp too late one night and was put in the cook-house as a punishment. When he was let out he came away with tea, chocolate and tins of food for us, hidden under his jacket. There were often parties at our house on a Saturday night, with the Land Army girls and the Americans. Someone played the accordion and there were sing songs and games of darts. I would creep downstairs to watch the dancing.

We were not badly off for food, as we were a farming family. Whenever a pig was killed we got a side of bacon which was hung behind the door with a coat over to hide it. We had chickens and ducks as well. There was plenty of milk and Grannie made butter. She cooked for six adults and four children. On Sundays she cooked a saddle of beef in the range and the vegetables were boiled in a muslin bag in the copper, with suet dumplings on top. We had regular visits from the doctor at school and he always said how well fed I was. I had my dinners at school. We each had an enamel plate and mug and we were made to eat everything. I hated liver then and I still do. There were always off duty Americans wandering round the town who used to give us sweets.

On the farm there was only one tractor and an old threshing machine. Grandad used horses and waggons. At harvest time, the corn was put into ricks, which my father used to thatch. Grandad was allowed to use a car as he was the manager of the brickworks at Market Lavington, but he only just got enough petrol for the business. My eldest uncle was a widower with five children, so he didn't get called up, neither did my father on medical grounds. I had two uncles in the Wiltshire Yeomanry, but the youngest was in the Medical Corps. Dad was in the Home Guard, watching for enemy planes from the roof of Blount's Court. One night when a shepherd was out with a lamp looking for stray sheep, the bombers must have thought it was a train and dropped a load of bombs. One made a crater in the road from Urchfont to Potterne. I used to get very frightened at the planes going over.

When the Italian POWs arrived, some were sent to work on our farm. They had to clear out the stream and remake the farm track which led from the road to the railway line. My cousins and I were told not to go near them but of course we did. Only a few of them spoke English. We were fascinated to see them making withy baskets and slippers from rushes. They used to plait the rushes to make the soles and weave them for the uppers. They also made rings from threepenny pieces (the old twelve sided sort) and sold all these things for pocket money.

I was sent to London when mother was ill to stay with my aunt. We went by train from Lavington which was a very busy station with the soldiers from the Plain and the boys from Dauntsey's School. I remember seeing the barrage balloons in London and I was surprised at the big tenements. Mother had saved my clothing coupons all year so I had a new coat and leggings. Mother was always knitting and she taught me. At school we used to knit blankets for the war effort. After the war we used our blackout curtains to make clothes and we used to buy parachute silk to make into petticoats. I didn't get to any of the victory parties because father was working on the farm and mother was ill.

Interviews by Lorelei Williams

How Devizes Won The War

GERMAN PRISONERS OF WAR AND A BABY

During the latter part of the war, German prisoners of war who were captured in France arrived by train to be sent to the prisoner of war camp on the London Road, marching along Rotherstone to avoid the Market Place where they were shouted at and spat upon. The distinctive tramp-tramp noise made by the marching column was a recognised sound, alerting mothers in the area to collect up their children playing in the street, and shut the doors, while peeping out at the Germans from behind lace curtains.

While Ethel Girvan was at the back of her house at number 5, she suddenly realised that the prisoners were on the march. After looking round for baby John, who was only crawling, she remembered that the front door had not been shut. She discovered that he had crawled into the road, right into the marching German column, which had to be halted while she retrieved him.

Most of the prisoners wore dirty and ragged uniforms, but many of them were happy to be out of the war and were treated better in the prisoner of war camps than on the war front. Older children would swop sweets for badges and buttons through the wire fence at the camp.

NEARLY SHOT IN DEVIZES

Bob Girvan, who lived with his wife at Rotherstone, was called up to work at the army barracks at London Road; being deaf and dumb and only able to communicate by signs, he was unable to go to the war front. He was a trained bespoke tailor and one of his jobs at the camp was to sew earphones into leather flying helmets as well as doing just about every other chore including loading coal. To enter the army camp he was issued with a permit pass, signed by the garrison Adjutant, but due to his popularity he usually only gave a wave to the guard at the camp entrance and did not show his pass.

One day in 1941, however, unknown to Bob, a new contingent of troops had moved in and a different soldier was on guard. On this morning Bob went through the gate, giving his usual wave without showing his pass. The guard challenged him, demanding to see his identity card. By now Bob had gone through the gate and kept walking without turning round. After several shouts, the guard raised his rifle, shouting, 'Halt or I'll fire!' But just as he took aim, another soldier turned up who recognised Bob and managed to push the gun away. And that's how Bob Girvan was nearly shot in Devizes!

John Girvan

British military and civilian personnel with American nurses at the London Road camp. Bob Girvan is second from the right

If you have enjoyed reading this book, why not join Devizes Local History Group? The annual subscription is £5 and new members are very welcome. Please contact Lorna Haycock (chairman) on Devizes 727369 for further details of meetings and activities.